WHAT PEOPLE ARE SAYING ABOUT

STILLNESS IN MIND

Simon Cole is a counsellor, therapist and meditation teacher...
with deep understanding of his subject.

He takes you on a journey to explain clearly the various levels
of meditation and how it can heal the stressed and busy mind to
move you into a much greater self-understanding... finding that
wonderfully peaceful and joyful "clear space" within.

A 'must read' for all that are interested in meditation.
Stafford Whiteaker in *The Good Retreat Guide 2014*, author of
Good Living in Hard Times: the Art of Contentment (O-Books),
Living the Sacred - Ten Gateways to Open your Heart (Rider & Co),
and *The Little Book of Inner Space* (Rider & Co)

I really enjoyed reading this book; it was refreshing to read about
mindfulness and meditation from a Person-Centred/Counselling
perspective... I found the descriptions and meditations acces-
sible and informative and the idea of linking breathing meditations with different mind states was useful, reminding me of
yoga pranayama... the description of self-actualisation was a
breath of fresh air and clearer than other ideas about development I have come across in meditation and psychotherapy...
the story of the Buddha listening to the wind was thought
provoking, leading the reader to ponder a little more and in an
unhurried way.

I would highly recommend the book to both introductory and
more advanced mindfulness practitioners.
Simon Carver MA, PMBACP, accredited counsellor and
psychotherapist

Stillness in Mind

a companion to mindfulness,
meditation and living

Stillness in Mind

a companion to mindfulness,
meditation and living

Simon Cole

CHANGE
MAKERS
BOOKS

Winchester, UK
Washington, USA

First published by Changemakers Books, 2014
Changemakers Books is an imprint of John Hunt Publishing Ltd., Laurel House, Station Approach,
Alresford, Hants, SO24 9JH, UK
office1@jhpbooks.net
www.johnhuntpublishing.com
www.changemakers-books.com

For distributor details and how to order please visit the 'Ordering' section on our website.

Text copyright: Simon Cole 2013

ISBN: 978 1 78279 739 5

A CIP catalogue record for this book is available from the British Library.

Design: Lee Nash

Printed and bound by CPI Group (UK) Ltd, Croydon, CR0 4YY

We operate a distinctive and ethical publishing philosophy in all
areas of our business, from our global network of authors to
production and worldwide distribution.

CONTENTS

For my family

Acknowledgements

This book draws on many years of working with people who were distressed and who have touched my life and I theirs. I have been affected, as they have, by our contact. So first I must acknowledge those (whose names I could not mention even if they were all still with me) – clients, students, voices, companions, fellow travellers, all of them part of the story.

In the introduction I mention the three intellectual giants behind my own philosophy and approach: Martin Buber, Carl Rogers and Eugene Gendlin. There have, of course, been many others, but for me these were cornerstones.

More specifically, and in relation to various versions of this book itself, I am indebted to my wife Janet, for an 'outsider' view at many points and to Diana Armstrong and Simon Carver, as established and successful therapists, for their time in reading and commenting cogently on more or less complete manuscripts, though errors and omissions are of course my own.

Finally I must thank the owner of the material who gave permission for its use as the example in the chapter "Clear Space" and whom I am unable to name.

Introduction

This work started out as a handout to follow my retreat courses in mindfulness meditation. Working from a centre to which people come for individual or group retreat, where they may stay from a few days to a few weeks, I have often felt, on the one hand, that I was never able to go far enough to set people off on the path of valuing a day-by-day meditation practice, while, on the other hand, I was conscious that I was 'rushing' in giving extra steps in order to better prepare them to continue when they left. I was also aware, particularly with our client-guests who came on individual retreat, that the 'before' and 'after' of the meditation sittings drew strongly on my background as a counsellor and psychological therapist. As a result, my idea of what I was writing started to evolve: the handout was starting to grow into a handbook, and then it felt as if it could be, not so much a manual of techniques, but a companion for a way of living.

What I would like you to find here, at the outset, is an everyday approach to a practice which is too fast becoming intellectualised on one level and trivialised by phone apps and the like on another – namely mindfulness – and then an invitation to move on from mindfulness into meditation, using a path which adopts a western therapeutic approach, in order to hold the link with day to day living. You will find chapters introducing mindfulness, and then the Clear Space Meditation Path and, because there is the opportunity to use this meditation path for personal growth or as an intentional therapeutic activity, I look at how we experience common emotional difficulties, relating them to this practice of meditation. After that I develop further the themes of mindfulness (particularly as an everyday intervention) and meditation, to bring in the new philosophy of living, which I believe can start to evolve.

The framework is that of a handbook, rather than a course or a technical treatise. However, for anyone wanting something more like a course, there are pointers to using it that way. It is difficult, when writing something like this, to pitch explanations at a level which would suit all possible readers. If, therefore, I have erred on the side of too much explanation of some terms for some readers, then I apologise; it was done in the interests of being as inclusive as possible.

I like to express things, as far as possible, in everyday language. For this reason you will not find any reference to *Pali* terms and only general references to Buddhism and its associated psychology. I acknowledge the deep connection between meditation and Buddhism, but I do not see it as a necessity to understand its processes and psychology in those terms. The practice of meditation can sit alongside a western philosophy of life and living and be expressed in such terms without losing anything of its spiritual nature and meaning. It can also be an accompaniment to psychological therapy of any kind. It does not cut across any precepts or practices of therapy; rather it 'loosens up' our awareness at an emotional level and can often provide 'data' in the form of insights or glimpses of enlightenment which can be worked with in a therapy session. So, if you come to this while you are engaged in counselling or similar, I would encourage you to welcome it and include it alongside the work you are already doing.

I chose not to arrange the chapters according to category. I wanted the experience for the reader to be one of a personal passage or journey, rather than a methodically arranged study. Thus, whilst most of the 'instruction' is in the first half of the book, the themed meditations, the theoretical chapters and the issue-related material are brought in according to how it seemed they were most likely to be of interest and relevance. To develop a mindfulness and meditation practice, it would not be necessary to first understand the concepts contained in the more theoretical chapter, "Being Still, Not Waiting" and "A Sense of a Self", but it seemed important to fully explain how the Clear Space Path brings together a meditation practice and a route to therapeutic personal development within a western cultural perspective.

Whether you are approaching this as an accompaniment to therapy or whether you simply want to explore the possibilities that mindfulness and meditation could offer you in your life, this companion is designed to allow you to progress at a pace that suits you. Whatever your reason, though, I suggest the following way to start. After you have glanced through the book to get an idea of what is on offer, read just the first two chapters, "Everyday Mindfulness ...", take a few days for each, and notice how the sort of things I have described come up for you day to day. Then start to practise 'intervening' in what is happening for you in the ways shown. None of the examples or anecdotes is going to exactly fit your experience, but I hope they will be close enough to enable you to use them as models. After a few days I think you will be acquiring enough sensitivity to the idea of mindfulness to be able to start to use it as the channel into meditation. Now is the time to read the next chapter, "Clear Space Meditation Path: Part 1" right through and then come back and work with it, successively starting to practise the steps it offers. You will note that this chapter refers to a period of six weeks over which the steps can be taken. At some stage during this, when you are comfortable with how your practice is developing, you might look through subsequent chapters, in particular "Being Ourselves and Visiting our Pain" and "Love and Its Confusions". These look at everyday emotions and relate them in a way which I believe you will find usefully informs and deepens your practice. I have not set out to offer an in-depth psychological study of these difficulties, but rather to frame an understanding about how we experience them, in a way which can be related to a Clear Space practice of meditation.

Interspersed with the instruction and the theory are four

themed meditations. I have introduced them where they seem to have some relevance to what follows or what has gone before, but that does not imply any prescription about how they should be used. They are not guided meditations or guided visualisations. They are intended to offer a nuance to your meditation, from time to time and when it is in tune with how you are feeling.

Whilst I have put forward this approach to using the companion, it is only one possible approach and, if your preference is to read right through something and then come back to work on it, then you should do what works for you. I recognise that for some people it is more comfortable to follow a course with set stages and a set rate of progression. However, I felt quite strongly that this was not the right way to set you on this journey. For journey it is, and where it takes you and what you encounter along the way will be unique to you. So I wanted to give you a starting point and a direction and allow you to meander along a path, which I believe will be growthful and emotionally deepening.

I have indicated what this approach is not (that it is not expressed in terms of Buddhist psychology), but it could be useful to briefly indicate what has been its inspiration. I would like to acknowledge three eminent lights in the field of philosophy and psychotherapy from whom I have drawn. Martin Buber was a philosopher and the prime mover in the revival of the Hasidic branch of Judaism. In his later life he lectured in anthropology and sociology at the Hebrew University in Jerusalem. I draw from him the insight he offers us into the process of human relating and the experience of presence. He is the sage in the story that appears at the beginning of the chapter "Being Still, Not Waiting". The inspiration of Buber will be detected also in the chapter "Love and Its Confusions", as well as echoes of one of his own influences, Søren Kierkegaard – though ...I must admit to having depleted the religious import of both their writings on the subject.

My grounding as a therapist is in the person-centred approach expounded originally by Carl Rogers. It was he who first introduced the notion of the sufficiency of the quality of the relationship in the therapy process, as being the principal ingredient for therapeutic change. From Rogers I take the nature of the relationship needed between therapist and client in terms of those qualities (known as core conditions) required of the therapist, but I apply them here in the context of the meditator's relationship with her or himself. From the same psychotherapeutic approach, I look to Eugene Gendlin, long time colleague of Rogers, who, without denying any of Rogers' philosophy or principles, developed a way of conceptualising the process of change and a method for directly stimulating the elements of that process. Gendlin's work has given me 'felt sense', which I use as "sense of" when talking about awareness in meditation. I also find great value in his insistence on the welcoming of each change step in perception, a practice we can apply to the shifts we sense in meditation as well.

To a synthesis of elements from these three eminent teachers I have added the concept of flow and the abiding possibility of incorporating all of what we are – our whole story – into each moment. Being present is also about achieving a transformation of our past as an element of our present, not simply a letting go, but a non-judgmental incorporation of where we have been, into where we are. In this way it does not distort our present awareness and, if we can learn to welcome all of who we are and what our story represents, then each moment can pass into the next in a way that is fulfilling and enlivening. To bring all these elements together, it seemed to need a shift in how we, at least from a western perspective, view the idea of self, and so I have 'grown' a new way of looking at and feeling our self, from the process of the book itself. You might think that would be a place to start, to define the self, but it seemed to fall elsewhere, and so you will find the chapter "A Sense of a Self" near the end and not at the beginning. It felt appropriate that an understanding of our self would be something we would come to... or perhaps we never do; perhaps it is always slightly ahead of us.

Bon voyage.

Simon Cole
Dardé, Ariège, France
November, 2013

I

Everyday Mindfulness and Mindfulness Every Day: Part 1

It could almost be said that too much has been said about mindfulness; that it appears so often, in the form of articles, presentations, books, phone apps, courses, that its all-pervading presence is a distraction. The problem with this is that distraction is exactly what mindfulness is not about. So I am going to say – at least to begin with – forget about mindfulness, and we'll work on not being distracted.

It is a truism that the modern world has far more distractions than former times, when the pace of life was slower, when information was not instantly available worldwide and when the choices which were presented to most people most of the time were quite limited. But if we are honest, it is really just passing the blame if we retort, "It isn't my fault; it's because there are too many things competing for my attention. You can't expect me to keep focused on one thing." That is projection[1] . Because the choice to attend to this or that, or even nothing at all, is ours alone. The cause of the distraction is not the extraordinary range of possibilities available to us but whatever it is about us that means we avoid making decisions, or, when we have decided and are set on a course and then see something else we want, we waiver. It is not difficult to detect what is happening – we always want the best we can get, but not just that, even when things are moving along nicely for us, if something appears which is faster, bigger, funnier, sexier, we have to check it out, just in case we might be missing something.

To avoid being distracted we need to understand how we think... because in our thinking patterns and what lies beneath them is where we will find the answer. So we'll start with a paradoxical question. What does it take to satisfy you? I could have asked, "What does being satisfied feel like?" But the two questions are really different sides of the same coin. So take something very mundane. Eating chocolate. You take one chocolate and eat it. Do you want another? You probably do. And another? Probably. But why? Will you get double the pleasure with the second one? If that is your reason, then you should consider the law of diminishing returns, because the second one can only possibly add fifty per cent to your pleasure and the third one thirty-three per cent, and so on. If you had only seen one piece of chocolate available and you had been asked after that piece whether you were satisfied, you would probably have said 'yes' because you would still have been savouring that piece. But if another piece had suddenly appeared, and you were asked if you wanted it, you would most likely have left off savouring the first piece and taken the second.

So, what does it take to satisfy you?

Eating is a good way in to mindfulness... in taking the second piece of chocolate, you were distracting yourself from savouring the first piece. Perhaps you want to wriggle out by saying that it wasn't you; it was the person who offered you the chocolate. But you cannot get away from the fact that it was you who turned your attention away from what you were doing, namely, savouring the pleasant taste in your mouth. So, allowing yourself to be distracted broke into your mindfulness in that moment. Why did you allow your attention to be drawn? Because there might be something nicer or better, or simply more, around the corner.

There is a Zen saying: when you are sitting just sit; when you are standing just stand; when you are walking just walk... above all don't wobble. It can be extended to any activity. In this context "just" is not solely about the physical action either; it extends to doing the thing without an attitude, that is, without bringing any particular guilt, desire, resentment, even indifference, to what you are doing. So, when you are savouring the taste of chocolate in your mouth, just do that. Don't even feel guilty because you are on a diet and you are not supposed to have chocolate at all! That would be your ego getting in the way. We could say it is about respect – respect for the moment. This moment will never come again, and a moment identical to this one will never again appear, so it deserves our respect for being a moment in our lives.

Most people eat too fast to really taste what they are eating. Very few people take the time to savour. Try this for yourself next time you are eating a meal. Notice how long you are actually registering the taste of the food. When you find you are thinking about something, notice how that means that you are not conscious of what you are eating, but simply of the act of eating, which has become a background activity, like driving a car while you are talking to your passenger. If you need help to slow down eating, try setting down your eating utensils as soon as you have put the food in your mouth and do not pick them up again until after you have swallowed the previous mouthful. That will help in another respect too, because it will mean that you cannot start preparing the next mouthful before you have finished the current one. To help yourself experience just eating, give yourself time to register everything about what you are eating – the texture... the flavour... is there just one texture? Is there just one flavour? (In the case of chocolate you could try closing your eyes and not biting, just letting it dissolve in your mouth. And then, out of respect for the moment, say to yourself "that was good and it is enough.")

Just one more thing about savouring: make sure that you note a flavour or a texture for what it is and avoid, if you can, a reaction of "that's not very nice" or "I don't like that." This is not because we have to like everything equally, but because telling ourselves that we don't like something will take us away from just eating and will have us make a judgement about the moment itself as well as what it contains.

So, the first step in mindfulness is not to get distracted.

The next step, which is closely related to it, is not to anticipate.

Whatever is going on right now, however good we are feeling, our instinct is to be thinking about the next moment, the next thing we might do. We anticipate. All the time. But supposing we took the risk not to. What would we lose and what would we gain?

Try out this visualisation:

> You are sitting comfortably in a chair at home reading a book which you are part way through and which you are enjoying...
>
> You are aware that your wife/husband/partner is going to be back sometime in the next half hour; it's a background awareness...
>
> You are absorbing what you are reading...
>
> You suddenly remember that you forgot to remind them to buy some more potatoes...
>
> Now you start to wonder whether that means you will have to go out again this afternoon because you will need them tonight with friends coming round and how soon will you have to go out because you said you'd be in to take a phone call unless you were to phone first but that might cause a bit of a problem at the other end...
>
> You notice you can't follow the beginning of the new paragraph in your book. You'll have to go back and read the last paragraph again...
>
> You hear your wife/husband/partner come in, you say a quick 'hello', and you ask straightaway if they remembered

the potatoes...

They are upset. *"Can't you see I'm in a mess because I fell over and tore the sleeve of my new coat, and all you can worry about is whether we've got enough potatoes?"*

Alright, so what in this example was lost by anticipating?

– concentration on what you were reading and connection with the narrative, and so needing to re-read;

– the possibility of an empathic (and sympathetic) greeting with your wife/husband/partner, and so some distance, and, for a while, some friction between you, until you could recover your connection.

What was gained?

– nothing

So, the next step in mindfulness is not to anticipate. To help you, there is a rule that you could give yourself, namely, stay with something until it finishes or you intentionally finish it. With the eating examples, you hadn't finished eating; you were simply letting something else go on at the same time. With the reading example, you could have decided to get to the end of the paragraph or chapter before letting your thoughts diverge. If there is no need to set a specific end, you could simply carry on with what you are doing (just doing it) until your attention is demanded elsewhere, and then you move your attention there.

It might seem, with all this attention on what is going on in the present, that it would be un-mindful if we allowed ourselves to do any planning, or working things out, or considering how we are going to do something which is due to come up later. But that need not be a difficulty, because to be mindful in that situation would be to be mindful that we were engaged in planning or working something out, and this was where we would hold our focus until it was needed somewhere else.

Perhaps it could be objected that such a challenge – to be

mindful all the time – is unrealistic because real life cannot be like that; it is too complex and many things have to happen at particular times. And yet, why not? Setting an internal reminder to look at the clock every so often would be fine, so long as, having looked at it, we then returned to what is in the moment. The test is whether we allow one moment to be encroached on (and contaminated!) by something that has no connection with it.

For now that is enough to be working with. We have been talking about 'everyday mindfulness' and focusing on mindfulness of activity. In the next part of everyday mindfulness we will look at how we bring distortions into our perception of what is going on in the moment, and then later we will look at mindfulness in relation to feelings and emotions.

Footnote:
1. The word used in psychological therapies for when we shift our discomfort onto others, most often by implying blame in some way.

2

Everyday Mindfulness and Mindfulness Every Day: Part 2

Jon Kabatt-Zin defined mindfulness as: "compassionate and non-judgmental awareness of the present"... so apart from not being distracted and not anticipating, we need not to make a judgement about the present moment in terms of what it is bringing us, and so to hold precious each moment for being a part of our lives.

To allow something to be what it is without needing to make a judgement runs counter to how we mostly run our lives. Most of the time we are making judgements. We make judgements about people's actions (she or he should or shouldn't have done that). We make judgements about others' opinions. (Do you really think that?) We make judgements about what we might do. (It's not worth spending my time just to get that!) And the list could go on. We spend so much time making judgements that we find it very difficult to let something be just what it is. We do that with people and things and ourselves, anything in fact that is part of the moment that is happening now. So what is going on?

Everything that comes in from our senses and everything we see that we are doing ourselves, our brain interprets – it is a part of making us conscious about what is going on. It interprets according to a frame of reference[1], which has been developing since the moment of our birth (many would say before), shaped by the billions of experiences which have gone into creating the person we are. Those experiences were ours alone, so our frame of reference is unique to us. This means that there is nothing neutral in the way we interpret.

A major challenge in our quest to be mindful is to set aside elements of our frame of reference and, in the interests of neutrality, to allow these stimuli from our real present to be just what they are, and no more, and then to value them for being that. In mindfulness terms nothing is negative and nothing positive because we cannot use those words without bringing in our own presumptions, and these are always away from the present moment. We also need to not construct any idea in our minds around what something is or what it means but simply to notice its existence in terms of how it presents itself to us – a kind of 'sitting alongside', rather than a 'looking at'. If we do this we free ourselves to respond to the real moment, unencumbered by the constraining framework which our brain uses to say what something "must surely be" – a framework which it modifies only very slowly, and, by definition, a framework which never contains the present moment, until it has passed.

Let's take an example to try. Close your eyes and wait for the first sound that you hear. You will probably notice that, as you heard the sound, you told yourself what it was and then probably registered whether it was pleasant, or just a noise, and then perhaps gave yourself a picture of the thing that was making it... and so on. All of that was coming from the schema that your brain uses for interpreting what it hears, but it was a long way beyond the 'just' I talked about in the last chapter. So now close your eyes again and wait for the first sound, whether you hear the same one or not, and this time as you hear it, stay with the sound itself and focus only on its nature, the modulations and resonances contained in the varying intensities of the air as it strikes your ear-drums.

If you were able to do this without letting your mind speculate in any way about the sound, then you were being mindful.

None of this means that thinking is banished when we come to mindfulness. If there is something that we are needing to understand or, as we said before, something that we are needing to plan, and we are focusing on that process, which is immediate and present, then we are being mindful. In this case, what we believe we are doing, what we are telling ourselves that we are doing, is what we are actually doing, and the brain is not wandering up all sorts of other alleyways.

Without getting too heavy, we could say that mindfulness is a discipline. It is not unrealistic to suggest that it is a way of being that we can aim to adopt all the time. I say "aim" because, being human, we will not completely succeed, but if we work at it, we can come close. The essential aspects of mindfulness which we have touched on so far are: to respect the moment (which also means being satisfied with the moment); to be aware of what is present in the moment and not make judgements about it; to allow things to be what they are and to notice all that is present for us.

If we are working towards always being mindful, we need to find a way to be aware when those things aren't happening. Our difficulty is that the mind we need to use to notice what is happening is the same mind that is the cause of a lack of mindfulness in the first place. It is its own fifth-columnist, you might say. Yet it is possible to use the mind to watch the mind. It is almost certain that when you are not being mindful, you are telling yourself stories; in other words, you are engaged in a train of thought which is re-playing old events, or elaborating on what is actually going on, or speculating or fantasising about something in the future. So it is the stories we need to spot. There is a way to do this which is rather like an app running in the background on a computer. The 'app' in this case is a question: "Am I intending what I am doing right now?" If your mind is following a train of thought such as I have just mentioned, the answer to that question can only be 'No'. In fact the answer is superfluous because by asking the question, you have already brought yourself back to the present. How often your 'mind app' pops up and prompts you is something for you to set, but just reading this will mean that you are conscious of it and, if you need more prompting, you could write out this paragraph and carry it with you.

"Killjoy!" I hear someone say, "I like day-dreaming," to which I would reply, "That's fine, so long as you know that you are day-dreaming." It is all in the intention. If we intend to do something, then we have made a decision to do it, and actually doing it is part of the present. The same goes for planning or analysing. If we are truly responding to a wish or a need, then we are carrying out an intention, and that is OK.

When you have worked with what I have put forward in these first two chapters and are starting to understand how you allow yourself to be distracted, how you anticipate, and how you judge, then you are in a position to start to use mindfulness as the channel to begin Clear Space meditation. So that is where we will go next.

Footnote:
1. "Schema" and "frame of reference" are terms used in psychology to refer to the amalgam of historical, social, cultural, experiential and perceptual information we retain and continually expand to be able to interpret everything we see, hear, feel – anything that happens to us in fact.

Clear Space Meditation Path: Part 1

Like all meditation paths, Clear Space needs a commitment to certain understandings from the meditator. We might call them the five precepts…

- a regular (daily) and patient attention to a period of sitting
- a preparation by lifting the burden of any expectations
- an understanding of not judging and not censoring
- a patience with an experience which will seem to fluctuate
- a welcoming of whatever transpires from each sitting

What is set out below is a progression along the path, a path that should not be rushed. How long is appropriate before any individual is working fully with everything contained here is impossible to say because we are all different and our experiences have affected us in different ways. So, because one person finds they take six months and another two means nothing in terms of the value and depth of experience for each. But it is unlikely that you could fully value all that is set out here and be effectively using this meditation path in less than six weeks of a daily practice which has built up to around forty minutes a day. And beyond this your practice will still go on developing. So I urge you to take your time as you step along the path and, from time to time, pause to look around.

A regular and patient attention to a period of sitting...
Your aim should be for the act of meditation to be approached as no more than "the next thing to do", without any decision-making involved. If we have gone through any deliberation of 'whether' or 'if' or 'when', even once we have decided and have sat in our meditation place, we will be carrying remnants of that decision and its alternatives in our head. Thus we will not be starting with Clear Space. An unexpected effect of developing a ritual is that it starts to become part of the definition of our day, so that there is some impetus, which would turn to an unsettled feeling, perhaps even disappointment, if we omitted it and our day did not fit into the mould we had given it. A time slot in the morning is generally preferable, with a period of meditation starting at ten minutes and increasing over a number of weeks to forty minutes.

A preparation by lifting the burden of any expectations...
Expectations always limit action and diminish our experience. If we carry an idea of the outcome we expect as we are engaged in the activity, we limit what we see (because we tend to see what we are wanting or expecting to see), and so we limit what we can allow ourselves to do and restrict the range of possible outcomes.

An understanding of not judging and not censoring...
When we make judgements, we are looking from a particular perspective. When we censor, the same is happening, except that the process is not fully conscious and what we censor out is usually excluded before it even comes into awareness. The effect of both is to narrow the field in which we are working. So, in the terms of the Clear Space metaphor, it would be like finding an open field in which we are told we have the freedom to roam and run and enjoy ourselves as we wish ... except for a fenced-off bit in the middle. Judging and censoring are the way we fence off and obstruct what needs to be clear space in order for the process of meditation to be truly creative.

A patience with an experience which will seem to fluctuate...
Each day is different, that is to say, each day we are different.
Identical tasks carried out at different times have a different
impact on our being – mind, body, spirit. The difference may be
too small for us to detect, but it will be there because nothing
stays still and the world is constantly changing. With the
heightened sensitivity which a meditative state brings, even the
smallest differences can be felt in their effect on our experience.
If we hold on to our intention not to judge, then no particular
session can be better or worse than another; it is simply what it
is, and the next one will be different again.

A welcoming of whatever transpires from practice and sitting...
This goes further than not judging. It is an intention to prize
whatever our experience has been. 'Prize', as a verb, is a slightly
old-fashioned word, but Carl Rogers uses it in talking about one
of the core conditions of a therapeutic relationship – a more
modern synonym might be to 'hold precious'. The "therapeutic
relationship", in our context here, is our relationship with
ourselves.

Mindfulness as the Channel

When using mindfulness as a channel for meditation we focus on
something that is present and immediate, and we let our mind
stay with that until it is no more than what it is. Most commonly
(and in the approach I set out here) we would use our breathing
for this because breathing is the ground of our being; though
really it does not matter what you use as a focus, and a candle, a
stone, a shell, or the greenness of the grass can all work.
Consistency, at first, is important.

The following is how we would use breathing as the
mindfulness channel. Try it out now and take your time over
each step.

First sit comfortably and relax any tensions you feel in different parts of your body... let the tension in your muscles go, perhaps by imagining them as strings on a guitar when the pegs are released and they become loose and limp...

Now take three long, slow breaths, being conscious of drawing the air right down to the bottom of your lungs, your diaphragm swelling slightly, and use these breaths to settle into a comfortable posture and let your muscles relax further...

After the three long breaths, gradually let your breathing subside and settle and, as you do this, notice any physical sensations connected with your breathing, such as the way your clothes move against your skin, the rise and fall of your diaphragm, the air cool in your nose or throat as you breathe in and slightly warm as you breathe out...

As you become aware of some physical sensations, notice that they have a rhythm, which is the rhythm of your breathing...

Allow your eyes to half-close and tune in to this rhythm, letting yourself feel it as a flowing, gently beating life-force carrying you along...

Relax into this feeling for a while and then, when you are ready, slowly open your eyes, look around you and bring yourself back into your surroundings.

Practise this a few times until you can achieve the progression without having to think of it as a succession of stages in the way that I have written it here.

Different Modes of Breathing

We can be affected by our breathing. I have described it as the ground of our being. It can alter the way we feel. It can alter our sense of ourselves. And in mindfulness meditation it is perfectly alright to have in mind how we want our breathing to be. Here are some ways of feeling your breathing, which you might move into at different points in a sitting, but remember that first it is important to steady and smoothe your breathing, watching to see that you are not holding onto it at any point and that the rhythm is even and the pace is comfortable.

breathing which strokes... as you breathe in let your muscles relax as if they are hanging in space, letting the incoming breath 'float' up into your body; as you breathe out let yourself 'lean' into your breath as it leaves, lightly smoothing out tissue and muscles – this is the stroking ... breathe slowly, taking longish, slow breaths.

breathing which slows... with medium-length breaths, first ensure that in and out breaths are the same length and then start to pause at the end of each in and out – your pause must be no longer than a second and need feel like no more than a slowing to turn round, like a pendulum at the end of each swing... you can let your picture of this be a kind of rounding, your breathing swinging slowly like the pendulum.

breathing which stills... here you will allow your muscles to relax with a sensation of weightlessness, as if you were simply a body floating in space and could feel no physical contact around you... feeling no contact you are yet connected to everything... you will notice your breathing become lighter and shallower until you barely have any sense of the breath passing... occasionally you may find you take an involuntary very deep breath, but this will not disturb the stillness.

breathing as a friend... this is your breathing as a steady beating pulse, the backdrop to everything, like the back of a chair you might lean against when you are tired... the sense of a support you can fall back on.

So in different ways we use breathing as an anchor. When thoughts have intruded, we can return our attention to breathing in order to come back to the clear space within us. Our breathing is always there. Obvious, yes, but for something so obvious it's surprising how much we take it for granted. In meditation from time to time we consciously take our awareness to our breathing, like turning to someone who has been standing in the background and whom we greet with "oh yes, I know you," as we re-join their company.

Thoughts as Clouds, and Leaves Falling...

We don't have to get far along any meditation path before we notice that, however good our intentions, our mind starts getting in the way and thoughts start appearing. Some might be linked to what we are doing and start giving us a commentary on it; others might be about things we've done or things we're going to do, people, worries, plans – anything in fact.

There is nothing abnormal about thoughts intruding. Our brain never stops and so needs to be trained by regular practice to be satisfied with letting us stay still and quiet and simply be. We have to accommodate the intrusion rather than fight against it because, if we fight against it, we set up another mental process doing the fighting, which takes us even further away from the possibility of clear space.

Thoughts are just thoughts, and we can notice them, acknowledge them even, and let them be what they are – wisps in our mind, like clouds in the sky, changing shape, being blown along, but always in the end dissolving and disappearing. Just like when we notice a cloud, we might notice its shape and its shade of white or grey, when we notice a thought, we might notice it being from the past, something we are re-playing, or from the future, something we are rehearsing or imagining, or something projected, something we are fantasising about. Just noticing the types of thought may be enough to dissolve them.

These are the thoughts we can allow to drift away like clouds. Another picture which you may find useful is to think of thoughts as leaves falling from a tree into a stream where they are carried away, sometimes slowly, sometimes faster, sometimes getting snagged on a branch or resting against a stone, but in the end being carried away by the stream's current.

* * *

Here is the framework for a meditation session starting with the mindfulness channel. As I have said, the time you allot could start at ten minutes and progress over a few weeks to forty minutes. It is good to acquire the ability to know where you are in terms of the length of time you have been sitting. It would be preferable not to glance at a clock every few minutes, and you should find after a while that you can tell yourself how long the session is going to be before you start and then come out naturally very close to that time. It is a facility that grows with practice.

When you are sitting in an alert but relaxed position and have taken a few moments to centre yourself, take three long, slow breaths (each time ensuring that you breathe out fully) to start to focus your attention inwards...

After the three long breaths, gradually let your breathing subside and settle and, as you do this, notice any physical sensations connected with your breathing, such as the way your clothes move against your skin, the rise and fall of your diaphragm, the air cool in your nose as you breathe in and slightly warm as you breathe out...

Now you are aware of some physical sensations; notice that they have a rhythm, the rhythm of your breathing...

Allow your eyes to half-close and tune in to the rhythm of your breathing, letting yourself feel it as a flowing, gently beating life-force carrying you along...

You are following the flow of your breathing as it carries you towards your clear space. Your clear space may be a visible open space in nature, or it may be the space of silence, or it may be the space in an open sky where you can stretch out your arms into emptiness – allow whatever comes up, whether it is an image, or a sense, or a feeling...

Relax in your clear space...

When a thought arises, just notice it and notice its nature – replaying, rehearsing, imagining, or fantasising, but no more. Allow thoughts to drift past like clouds, change shape, perhaps join another, but always dissolve into the air under a clear blue sky...

If you have difficulty with allowing the thoughts to just float away, return to your breathing, feeling its flow like a life-force carrying you along...

Allow yourself to really feel your clear space in the form it takes for you ... notice space, openness ... notice where in your body responds to your clear space, perhaps an extreme feeling of relaxation in all your muscles, perhaps a soft tingling at the base of your spine...

When the time feels right, start to lengthen your breathing until you take three long, slow breaths and, as you do so, open your eyes fully and return to the room.

This is the first stage of the Clear Space Meditation Path. It needs practice until you can comfortably do this and no more, for at least twenty minutes.

Felt Sense – Beyond Thinking...

Less specific than thoughts there are other awarenesses which lead us to the 'felt sense' of something. They may at first seem like thoughts themselves, but they will be much more connected with the present moment – they might be very mundane like noticing that your foot is itching, or they might be much more vague, but equally real and very present. These are the ones which will form an important part of how we develop our meditation later. You may notice yourself becoming aware of 'my work', 'my family', 'my being shy'. You could turn your attention to any of these and start to describe them, see a picture of them, tell stories about them, but, if you do none of those things, they can still have a presence in your mind. It is this presence in your mind, without any concrete description or picture, that we will call the 'felt sense' of a thing. Whenever I talk about this sense, I am always meaning the 'sense of you and this person or thing or part of you'.

Try an exercise now to recognise this 'felt sense'. Take something or someone close to you in your life, quite possibly one of your family. We'll say you take your mother (and it does not matter whether she is alive or not). Most likely she will appear with some fairly concrete form in your mind. Now shift your mind to the feeling you associate with "you and her". Don't bring up a photo, don't hear a voice, don't tell a story, just stay with the "you and her" feeling. Underneath will be all sorts of memories, voice clips, and images, but stay with the "you and her". This way it is the "sense" of her which is with you. It is this 'sense of' a thing which we shall work with later in part two, because it can be taken beyond people into aspects of our life and aspects of ourselves.

If you have difficulty with developing or recognising this 'felt sense' of something, try this – taking the example of your mother again. Imagine yourself sitting with her in a room you both know, but not at any particular time or doing anything in particular, just sitting with her. As you imagine yourself there, notice any feelings that come up, being there with her. When a feeling comes, name it (but don't start telling a story) and check to see whether the word you have found completely represents everything about 'you and your mother'. If it doesn't, go back to sitting with her in your mind and wait for another feeling to come up and do the same. You might also notice glimpses of typical images or sounds or ways she comes into your mind. These can also be part of the sense of you and her, until in the end you have a whole collection of these 'glimpses' of your mother which go to make up the sense of 'you and her'.

Another method you might try to help you get to this sense of something is by drawing. Take a plain sheet of paper and some pencils or crayons. Think about the person close to you and everything about the relationship you have with this person – feelings, events, life circumstances, history, everyday things between you. Now represent these in a drawing – not with a picture of the person but with these images of your relationship with them. Don't worry about your drawing skills – this is not meant to be fine art! When you have finished and you are satisfied that you have depicted everything you can bring to mind about 'you and her/him', set your picture up a little way away, far enough so that when you look at it, the individual parts of it don't really stand out, and what you see instead is a composite image or picture. Spend a few moments just looking. This is a visual version of your 'sense of you and the other person'. When we come on to using 'felt sense' in meditation, you could, if it helps to begin with, put a picture you have created a little way away and, when you are sitting in meditation, open your eyes enough to look at it for a few moments in order to prompt the 'felt sense of ...' while you are meditating.

This 'sense', as we are talking about it here, is an important part of the Clear Space Meditation Path, and so it will repay the time you give now to really understanding how you can go to it and what it is like when you are able to touch on it. When you use it in meditation, the 'sense of you and...' might be a person, but it could equally be an object, an animal, a situation, an aspect of your life, the way you are in certain circumstances, an aspect of your personality, your feelings about something, almost anything, in fact, which is linked to you and which affects you.

When you are ready, extend your meditation in this way:

You have followed your breathing as it carried you towards your clear space. You have relaxed in this space. Thoughts may have appeared, and you have been able to notice them as no more than thoughts and let them float away. And between the thoughts you are able to notice more and more your body responding to space and openness...

As you wait, notice especially any thoughts, which are not past or future, but come from present awareness. From these 'thoughts' will develop your 'felt sense' of something. As before, your sense of something/someone is always "you *and* it/them"...

As a sense develops, simply allow it space; so don't 'look' at it or attempt to describe it, but simply know it as it develops, as you 'sit alongside'...

You will notice that in this way your sense can be with you and be in its own space, so that you can return your awareness to your clear space and wait there as before. You may find you unwind with a feeling of profound relaxation; or you may move towards your sense again, notice that it is still close, and then return; or you may notice that a different awareness arises which starts to develop into a new sense...

When the time feels right, leave the meditation as before.

If you are meditating with someone to whom you are close, and you are aware of their presence as the sitting starts, you are quite likely to find that it is the sense of them which comes up first. The same principle applies. Allow the sense of you and the other person to develop, but don't start telling yourself a story about them, or even telling yourself what you feel for or about them; simply hold the sense of them, their presence, like the silhouette of a flower inside a part-opened bud.

If you have followed what I have set out and have developed a regular sitting practice over a period of four weeks or so, then you have made good progress down the Clear Space Path. Do not rush to start on the second part of the path until you feel you are making good progress. Perhaps, if you are reading this book right through, even though your practice may not have moved beyond the level of this chapter, spend some time on the chapters which are not specifically about the meditation method, as you keep practicing with this chapter, and then come to the second part when you feel you have made progress here.

Some Practicalities

Hints about Posture and Sitting

The Lotus or Half Lotus positions or even sitting cross-legged on a low stool or cushion are not essential ingredients of good meditating posture. If you are not able to sit with legs crossed for any period of time due to injury or lack of physical flexibility, then sitting in a straight chair is quite all right. What is important is that your back should be erect, with the weight of your head and torso being passed down your spine through your pelvis to where you are sitting, and ultimately through to the earth. Thus you will be grounded – metaphorically and literally. To help your spine stay straight, it is a good idea to check that your hips are on a level or even slightly higher than your knees. Most people find that, even though they might start with an erect spine, they gradually allow it to curve, so from time to time you may find it helpful to pull your spine back to the upright.

Your eye line should be horizontal, and as you take your first breaths you can allow your eyes to half-close, which will mean that you are not looking at anything in particular, but that you have a little light to keep you alert.

You will see that the essentials of this posture can be achieved in an upright chair with a fairly firm and level seat. The intention is that your posture should help you to stay alert but not impose distracting discomfort. Hence lying down is unlikely to be an appropriate position, unless it is a physical necessity, because of the difficulty of staying alert when in this position.

To help you relax as you begin, use your breathing, gently becoming softer and shallower, to carry away the tensions in your muscles. There is a close link between our psychological 'busy-ness' and what we feel in our bodies. Sometimes we can be so wound up that our body feels as if it is taut and quivering from the stress of pent-up tensions. This needs to be discharged before useful meditation can begin. A picture can help.

Imagine a pool into the middle of which a stone has just been thrown. Ripples spread out from where the stone entered the water. At first they are quite big, almost like waves, and close together; then, as they move away towards the edge, they gradually space out and become gently undulating movements on the surface until even these all but vanish as they reach the bank. Finally the surface of the pool is completely still. As you look at this picture in your mind, let the tension your mind has brought to your body ebb away, draining out through your limbs and feet and hands and finger tips, like the ripples disappearing as they reach the edge of the water. As you begin to relax you may notice your tongue detach from the roof of your mouth and float, giving a feeling of space opening up; and you may notice yourself swallow involuntarily as you move into a meditative state.

To help you to return to your clear space when you have experienced more than passing thought intrusion, you can turn back to your breathing and start again to follow its flow. As an additional help to calm tension you might lengthen your breaths and be more conscious of your out-breath than your in-breath, even noticing the passage of air through your nostrils and allowing yourself to hear its sound and to feel its motion like a gentle stroking of your body. (I referred to this before as "breathing which strokes".)

To help you when you feel drowsy, you can raise your head slightly so that your eyes are above the horizontal.

To help you when you feel the clamour of too many sensations, lower your head so that your eyes, if they are open, are looking at the floor in front of you. At the same time become more conscious of your breathing and pause very briefly at the end of each in- and out-breath. You may find that this will give you a sensation of 'rounding', which will have a calming effect. (I have referred to this previously as "breathing which slows".)

When you are ending your meditation, take time to let your full consciousness come back, in particular moving back into your clear space and allowing yourself some moments there, starting to feel again your surroundings, before you begin to lengthen your breaths and fully return.

Contemplation After Meditation

It is important to allow yourself a few moments after your meditation, in a different position but without moving too far, to be with your experience of this new kind of peace and to nurture any awareness which has arisen. There is no prescription for this, but you might try something along these lines:

As you are coming back into the room, still sitting, slowly uncross and straighten your legs...

At the same time stretch your arms out beside you and then gently raise them above your head until your palms meet...

You might stretch and then relax a couple of times...

Now bend until your arms are reaching out along your straightened legs with your fingers pointing towards your toes, allowing your torso alternately to stretch and relax so that your fingers make contact with your toes if you can...

Notice the contrast between the tension in your legs (your hamstrings and calves) and the release you can bring to your arms and upper body as you rest the muscles in your arms...

Pause there for a few moments, then slowly gather your legs in at the knees with your arms until you are sitting loosely 'coiled up' with your head bowed over your knees...

Stay for a couple of minutes like this, feeling the comfort of your body turned in on itself in repose, holding the memory of your meditation experience, the senses which have come to you and the feelings from within you which have met them...

This description assumes you have been sitting crossed-legged, but it can be adapted if you have been sitting in a chair. You will not be able to gather your legs up in the same way, but you could still stretch your arms out beside you and above you and then bend your head over towards your knees, resting your forearms on your legs in front of you.

That is the physical aspect of leaving your meditation.

But there is a mental aspect too. To keep a record as your practice develops can also be useful. For this, a meditation journal can help you to recall themes that recur in your meditations and allow you to reflect on changes as time passes and your practice develops. No need for a detailed narrative; just headlines, senses and feeling responses are sufficient.

Distractions

We have already talked about thoughts and their intrusion into the clear space to which our breathing can lead us, but we can be subject to other distractions too. The source really comes from within us, although it may seem to come from outside. I am thinking in particular of intrusive noise. Now, on one level we might say that it is part of the present moment, of which we need to be mindful. But I am not talking about the noise itself, rather the way our mind can sometimes hook itself onto a distraction like noise in an almost obsessional way. It is as if the mind has lost touch with the body by removing itself into the noise and is then unable to escape. If this happens it will certainly sabotage the meditation process and will probably lead to physical tension. If you experience such distraction it will be useful to visualise it in the way I have described – the mind losing touch with the body – and then to bring into awareness whatever physical sensations go with your sense of being grounded, thereby recovering your mind back into your body, being supported by the earth and noticing where you feel these sensations in your body. Confirm this awareness to yourself and spend some moments 'wallowing' there and feeling the full and pleasing effect.

Difficulty with Motivation

As with many things, which we know are "good for us" but where the rewards are not immediate, it can be difficult to make meditation a regular activity. Perhaps initially, because it is something new and curiosity gives you a kind of buzz about it, you have a burst of activity with it, but too soon discomfort, or boredom, or lack of results, or embarrassment, or disillusion, or a combination of all these takes over before the habit is fully formed.

In the early stages, there is no substitute for willpower. But you can do things to increase your chances of maintaining your practice.

First, decide when you are going to sit in meditation; a regular time of day - daily is preferable - and a usual place are both important. If that means setting an alarm then that is what you should do, whatever the time of day, though early-ish in the morning, before or immediately after breakfast, is a good time. At the end of the day can work when you are more experienced, but initially you may find yourself getting drowsy.

Secondly, there is no need to be too ambitious about time. Decide on a plan; ten minutes is ample for the first week, then increase by five minutes per week until by week 7 you are meditating for around forty minutes.

Thirdly, it will take you about two weeks to develop the habit to the point where you would miss it if you didn't do it. It is during these first weeks when your will-power will be tested the most. You can make a deal with yourself at the time you decide that you are going to embark on meditation. As well as deciding to do it, formalise the decision in your mind by saying: "This is a decision which is binding and not up for review for at least two weeks." Now, when the time in the day comes, you simply do it because it is the next thing on the schedule, and it is not up for discussion. The only thing in your mind is the action itself, and any thinking about it is not on the agenda.

At the end of two weeks of consciously applying will-power, I hope that you will find that you look forward to your period of meditation. By then you might find that, when you finish, your impression of the time you have been sitting is less than the time you have actually taken, though consistent with what you intended.

After all this, it could be that it is still 'not working' because you are finding yourself excuses or you are not really clearing a space in the day for meditation – in one way or another you are avoiding. Don't despair and don't give up. Avoidance can give us insight. Ask yourself a question. The obvious question might be, "Why am I avoiding this?" But a better question would be, "What am I really avoiding?" The answer will most likely not be the practice of meditation itself. It is more likely to be something that meditation will make different if it becomes part of your life. And then the question becomes, "What is it about me and [this thing] that means I avoid taking this step?" And if you can answer this, then you are on the track of what you need to change in your thinking in order to make a regular practice of meditation possible for you.

Everyday Mindfulness and Mindfulness Every Day: Part 3

There is another aspect of mindfulness, which warrants separate consideration, namely mindfulness of feelings and emotions. The principle of compassionate and non-judgmental awareness is the same as before, but for many this is more difficult because, on the whole, we are less used to knowing what we are feeling than what we are thinking. In addition, in everyday conversation we often say, "I feel..." when in reality it is something we are thinking. There's nothing wrong with that, but for clarity here, it would be useful to separate the two. Here is an example. Supposing we had been talking about how things were going at work for you, and I asked you how you felt about you and your job. If you answered "I feel that my boss could give me a bit more leeway," you would really be giving me what you thought about it. If you had answered, "I feel a bit limited," then you would be giving me your feeling.

There is another barrier to being mindful of feelings. In the same way as occasionally we might put thoughts out of our head because they represent ideas we are ashamed of or don't want to believe that we could entertain, we do likewise with feelings... but probably more so. With feelings we can sometimes even banish what we would like to be feeling, as well as what we do not want to feel.

Try this exercise before you read on:

Ask yourself the following questions, pausing after each, and listen for the answers you give in your mind.

"What am I doing right now?"
"What am I thinking right now?"
"What am I feeling right now?"

Now replay your answers to each question and listen to them as if you were an honest but caring friend. Listen for where you have answered rather quickly or where you hesitated or where you changed your answer to get a "better" word. These are the places where you censored or where you judged.

Now try the same questions again, only this time you will have in your mind how you censor and how you judge, and you could decide not to so that you simply accept what comes up. When you have finished, replay your answers again in the same way. There is no-one listening except you, so you can take the risk of being true to yourself.

This is a good exercise to do from time to time in order to get used to finding feeling words. It is also useful to notice which feelings make you most uncomfortable when you find them and which you try hardest to make be something else. As you do this, realise that you are engaged in a process of familiarisation and that it is possible to be more at ease with how you are and what you are feeling. It doesn't mean that you like what happens or like what you do which ends up with your feeling this way. Neither does it mean that you might not decide to do some things differently in order not to feel certain feelings. It simply means that this is what it is right now.

Mindfulness of feelings and emotions moves us towards much greater self-understanding. We might not like coming face to face with some aspects of how we are, but we can feel relief from being honest with ourselves. It allows us to be constructive and work with where we are, something it is simply not possible to do if we are not open to our feelings. Until we are mindful, we are not really seeing what is going on, and so we will only accidentally do what is truly in tune with the person we are. We might look at it in this way: when we are not mindful we are constructing a kind of alternative reality around us, which we can make work (probably), but the overall effect is like a film where the sound is not quite synced with the picture.

Mindfulness of feelings is about making that connection and touching what you experience as the feeling. It is not really necessary to name it (and I have already talked about the 'sense' of things), but until you are used to noticing this 'sense of', it could help to give a name to the feeling to ensure that you are not avoiding a true awareness. It could be that feeling words do not come easily to hand. If this is the case, take some time to write out all the feeling words you can think of, perhaps arranging them into columns of mainly pleasant and mainly unpleasant. Then, when you think you've finished, try searching on the internet with the search term 'feeling words' – there are a lot more than you think!

Some time spent on what I have suggested in this chapter will be worthwhile preparation for moving further along the Clear Space Path.

6

Being Ourselves and Visiting Our Pain

There are ways in which we can use mindfulness and meditation to help deal with the difficult emotions to which we are all subject at times in our lives. On its own it is not a substitute for other therapeutic approaches, such as counselling, for under-standing and dealing with the issues which lie behind persistent and painful emotions, but it is often a good complement to counselling, with insights flowing between the two domains and enriching both processes.

At the end of this section I will offer a way to approach physical pain in the course of meditation, but first I want to set out some ideas about how the most common and persistent painful emotions arise and what it is that determines their intensity, their power in some cases to limit how we function, and their capacity to endure if not addressed. I am not seeking here to give a compre-hensive psychological analysis but to offer an understanding of the feelings and the processes that give rise to them, in a way that complements how we might approach them in meditation.

Attachment... is the psychological process which lies at the heart of most human suffering. It is a standard Buddhist teaching that "all suffering comes from clinging on". The use of 'clinging' in this translation is deliberate, in that it indicates something that is dysfunctional, an act of desperation, a sign that there is more at stake than appears on the surface. There is nothing wrong with attaching, so long as there is nothing wrong with un-attaching, but to cling on to something or someone when it/they have ceased to be a sustaining or creative force in your life implies some hidden owing or dependency which in the end will cause more distress.

All of the emotions I look at below owe something to the process which we know as attachment.

Disappointment... can be a momentary thing, or it can be more extended and might be a layer of feeling contained in emotions such as sadness or regret. It always relates to something that isn't but might have been. It is quite often accompanied, in our thoughts if not in our words, by "If only...". In origin the word relates to not having been appointed to a position, and so we can see that, giving it an emotional context, it implies not being in the (emotional) state that we expected to be. Thus it is not so much being deprived of something that in some way we possessed and have become accustomed to as being deprived of something that we expected. You will recall that the second of the precepts for the Clear Space Path for Meditation related to not burdening ourselves with expectations. And the implication of feeling disappointment is that, rather than simply wishing or hoping for something, we have expected it. Therein lies the pain that we feel – not acute perhaps, but still there – tied up with the emotional investment we have made in an outcome over which we did not have complete control, or maybe any control at all. A more mindful attitude to a future prospect would be: "If it happens, it happens." Of course there are still the times when the disappointment is with ourselves or with our part in something. The equivalent attitude in this case might be: "If I can do it, I will do it; if I don't manage it, it was beyond me." Does that sound insufficiently resolute? After the event it is simply a statement of reality. I suggest the lack of resolution, if there is any, comes in what we do next.

Sadness... can be with you and live with you like no other emotion, seeming to be able to coexist with whatever else may be going on, even though its source may be somewhere else entirely. Sometimes sadness is like a prison where the bars are enough to hold you in, but not so heavy that the outside world is hidden from view. You might even be able to share the normal life of others, but always you know that it is not your world, as if there were an invisible screen separating you from what is around you. Sadness accumulates, wearies, saps at the spirit, like nothing else. But then it can reach a point where there is nothing more it can take away, and it seems to become part of how life is. So we go on functioning, but all of our vitality has gone: every positive, every happy experience is damped by its weight. Life has become a flat line.

Sadness comes from compassion... for others, for ourselves, for what has never had a chance to be. Always there is this: if what happened had been otherwise, then a better future could have been enjoyed. In all sadness we hear the words "if only". With those words comes a belief in a possible alternative future for its own sake. We have become hostages of the unknown and unknowable.

In so many aspects of our life we have an attachment to things how they are. This goes beyond quite naturally wanting the things that we enjoy to continue, beyond the mindful awareness and appreciation of what is with us and gives us pleasure. This attachment is like pulling in to the present the enjoyment, pleasure, and comfort, which rightly belongs to the future. The process of attaching is making future happiness depend on the unrealistic condition that life will continue exactly as it is now. Like the investment banker who buys futures at a price that will show a profit if prices move in the direction he expects and is left with a loss if they don't, we invest our expectations in a future which is at least as good as the present, and then we cannot recoup when life takes a different turn.

So here is the challenge: to allow 'now' to be complete and sufficient in itself. And if it is complete, it is finished. Then tomorrow's joy, as it comes, can be tomorrow's and owe nothing to today.

Regret... because of something we have done, because of something we did not do, because of what we said or left unsaid... and right now it seems that, if we could go back, everything could be different, better. Regret, remorse, and guilt seem to overlap, but here it might be useful to look at what distinguishes each. Perhaps regret feels the least intense of the three, and maybe that is because it is concerned most often with how we have inflicted suffering on ourselves. So, I regret having been offhand with that colleague because it was not consistent with the person I believe myself to be. In this way I have let myself down, and so I feel disappointed in myself. How do we resolve something we are putting on ourselves? We are both persecutor and persecuted at the same time. If the persecuted 'me' is let off the hook, the persecutor 'me' has less to believe in, is less of a person because of lower standards. In the end this would be a route to a lower self-esteem. But if the persecutor wins the day, and I continue to be down on myself, then that too in the end is a route to lowering self-esteem. Catch 22. In the end the only way out is: to regret but... After the 'but' should come the statement of one's mindful awareness of oneself now, which contains all experience and learning up to this moment. In this moment I can say that I have an understanding of who I was, and the person I am now has grown from there and learnt from the experience. Now the persecutor can be satisfied and the persecuted can gain assurance.

Remorse... we feel because of what we have done which has hurt someone else. The word 'remorse' comes to us from Latin via French, and its origin means 'to come back and bite again' or, more succinctly, to torment. It is not about something we did to our own disadvantage; rather it is always about difficulties or suffering that we caused for someone else. It is distinct from guilt, being something that was thoughtlessly or carelessly done, without awareness and with no anticipation of harm. Remorse is more difficult to handle than regret. It is something we have done to another, and so it is something which has affected their happiness since we cannot, as with regret, take responsibility for the process and come to understand that all experience contributes to learning. In other words, we cannot 'regret but', on behalf of someone else.

In resolving issues, which cause difficulty, perhaps pain, we always have to remember that we only have ourselves to work with. It is true that we might be able to discuss something with another, even persuade them. In the realm of opinion and reasoning and action, this might have an effect. But in the realm of feeling and emotion it will have no effect. We cannot make someone like us; we cannot make someone feel happy. Perhaps we can act towards them in a way that helps their previous feelings subside, but whether that happens depends on them. And when it comes to remorse, the same problem is in us. We might say we are sorry for what we did, we may ask for forgiveness, and they may forgive us, but that on its own will not work. In the same way as we cannot make someone feel good about us, they cannot make our remorse go away even by forgiving us. We have to forgive ourselves. This seems like a paradox. But the remorse resides in us. If I say I am sorry to the friend I have wronged (which is something I should do anyway), his anger may be diminished, it may be extinguished to the point where he is able to say "I forgive you," and that will help him, but will it make a difference to me? If I am really feeling remorse (as opposed to anxiety because our friendship is threatened), then it will only help me if I can echo his forgiveness with my own.

Forgive ourselves... but how? Believe that the person I am now does not have to be the person I was before. Realise that my history can be my guide, my counsellor, my well-wisher even; I do not have to feel it as my accuser and my judge. When there is nothing that can be changed, to acknowledge is enough. To acknowledge confirms our faith in the present and in the sufficiency of the present. To do otherwise would be a betrayal.

Guilt... the word which has come down to us from old English, in which its early predecessor meant 'to pay for', as with a debt. So we can think of guilt as the payment for something that is owed, or as the outcome of something being owed but not paid. There may have been something that we have knowingly done, or, more likely, something we have knowingly failed to do, which has caused harm to someone else. It was contrary to our moral standards, but this did not stop us. Perhaps we did not expect it to cause significant distress, or perhaps we rationalised our need to do it, or perhaps we simply blocked from our mind the possible consequences... but now in some way it feels like there is a debt to be paid, a need to make amends.

In many cases, guilt can be relieved with the cooperation of the person who has been wronged – to feel and express genuine sorrow for harm caused can often help; to undo the damage caused, if it is possible, is a tangible sign of contrition. But always, if the recompense is not accepted or if circumstances do not allow, the possibility, then, is that we may have to live with an un-requited sorrow for our past action or inaction. But sorrow, if it is known and accepted, is a step because it is in the present and need not be displaced into other dysfunctional emotions and behaviour.

However, there is another way in which guilt manifests itself, which I shall call 'existential guilt'. In fact, this takes two forms. The first draws on a present feeling from a present perception; the second relates to a present feeling where the perception is about the past.

The sense of the first is of a feeling of guilt that I should even be alive. It need not relate to any act committed. There need not be anyone who has been wronged. The sense is more that of 'undeservingness', and at its root there is usually a comparison being made. So, I might feel undeserving because I am well off and there are so many who are not, or I might feel undeserving because what I contribute to my family, society, or humanity is so much less than others. But it also might be more vague, that I am undeserving of being alive because life is for living and doing and I am just coasting, and, in all other respects, I am content with that. And then I feel guilty about feeling content about it. In this form of guilt, what is 'owed but not paid' does not relate to others but to ourselves, more specifically our values. It is our values – to which we have an allegiance, even if they are largely handed down to us – with which we are in conflict, and we are on both sides. We could say that our would-be contentment is in conflict with our sense of duty and both, when unfulfilled, will generate negative feelings. It seems like a conundrum. One of two things would have to change. Either our philosophy of life, of which our values are a large part, has to be modified, or we must forego our expectation that life should be a largely comfortable experience. Otherwise we live with our discomfort. There is no cure, but patience with developing an attitude of mindfulness and a practice of meditation will help in bringing clarity.

The second form of existential guilt is about something we owed to ourselves. It arises when we discover that we have allowed our life to be impoverished by acting in a way which has not given us happiness, and that it was unnecessary. In retrospect we can say that we owed ourselves something better. If I have lived all of my life doing jobs which were un-stimulating and offered no prospects because I had left school without qualifica-tions, and then in my fifties, as a mature student, I obtain a degree in a subject which interests me and obtain a job which fulfils me, I may look back and blame myself for accepting the judgements of others and not trying to do better right back in my youth. The guilt I would feel would be towards myself for not gaining a better life for myself all these years. And in this way my guilt, which is about something in the past and cannot be changed, is detracting from my enjoyment of the present. So now I am paying twice, when at most only one payment was necessary. I say "at most" because the other thing I am doing is focusing on one theme in my story, when in fact there are many themes. The person I am now was not just the product of this one part of my life but of all the parts, and the person who has started to find fulfilment has been enabled to do so by all the parts of his life, by the sum of all his experiences.

Jealousy... starts from self-centredness. To be self-centred, at least some of the time, is natural and human. Some people are more so than others by nature, and some are more often than others according to circumstance. But none of us avoid it all of the time. Self-centred is not the same as selfish. Self-centred has its positives as well as its negatives. It can be protective. But it can also be wounding – wounding to others. Jealousy also wounds but only ourselves. It makes two assumptions: that what I don't have, I am entitled to and that what I want should not give benefit to another. In the realm of romance, it says that if I feel for someone, my feelings should be reciprocated, and that no-one else should have similar feelings for this person, however genuine. In the realm of possessions or achievement it is similar: whatever appeals to me should be available to me, and no-one else can have any entitlement until I am satisfied. Self-centred is veering towards selfish. Jealousy is complicated as well as destructive. It turns our focus inwards and reinforces our ego. It consumes a huge amount of mental energy. It obstructs relation-ships, whether that is with people in our lives or people who might come into our lives, or whether it is with life itself. It is the very opposite of mindfulness. That is not to say that mindfulness excludes being mindful of what we are feeling – we looked at that in the last chapter – but jealousy is not simply a feeling. Jealousy is hurt overlaid with inappropriate attachment, and it is the attachment element which is destructive. If we can allow ourselves to feel the hurt, just the hurt, then we can get past our jealousy, because our attachment is causing us to project our hurt as resentment, and possibly even hate, onto others. By projecting it onto others, refusing to own it ourselves, because we want to dull the pain, we make it impossible to resolve.

The way we approach this along the Clear Space Path is to go towards the hurt we feel, our pain – the opposite of our instinctive response – but more of that at the end of this chapter.

Anger... should be distinguished from temper and irritability and being cross or 'out of sorts' – it is altogether more substantial in psychological terms. Perhaps losing our temper might cause more problems with others, but temper is a behavioural response to frustration, which may have links with underlying anger, but is an outcome of inappropriate or unheeded boundaries and a lack of awareness. Anger, however, may be directed (either in thought or by action), or it may be felt as an emotion sitting somewhere inside us, not understood, or only partly understood. Whichever way, it takes up a lot of emotional space and uses up a lot of mental energy.

Underlying all anger is hurt. If we can recognise the hurt then we will be able to understand the anger. If we can relieve our pain and start to heal the wound, then we will reduce our anger. Generally, when we are wounded, it is by something outside our control. We can wound ourselves, but then we feel regret or guilt. When the wound comes from outside, we feel anger. A natural response is to lash out, physically or metaphorically, like some tormented animal. But reason can tell us that revenge does not work, that it is a palliative only, if it is even that. The response back from the other side might be retaliation, or it might be submission, the former risking pushing us further up the anger escalator, the latter prompting guilt at our intemperate reaction. Revenge is also a trap in another way. It carries with it a claim of being morally right. It is self-justification. The trap is that it holds us in our anger because we become preoccupied with how we are right and insensitive to our own feelings, when what our wound needs is attention and care. That part of us which feels the pain needs acknowledgement for its pain... it needs empathy. The possibility with our path of meditation is to recognise hurt without fighting the cause of the pain. With an attitude of mindfulness, we can acknowledge the pain as how we are feeling it, perhaps acute, but no more than pain. And then we can move towards it, as I explain below. This opens the way to responding to the pain as pain and, gradually, to a shift in our awareness, as the process of empathy starts to heal the wound.

Implied by the explanation I have just given is that the cause of the hurt, which has prompted our anger, is fairly explicit, even visible. But some anger is more like the rumbling of volcanic disturbance underground, always threatening to erupt, always menacing. The origin may be buried deep, and the source of the hurt difficult to find. The meditation path will ease the pain, but it is important to recognise when more is needed and to look for counselling or psychotherapeutic help.

Anxiety... is a human condition; few people can say that they never experience anxiety or that there is no aspect of their lives in which, at least in some circumstances, they would not feel anxious.

It is helpful to distinguish anxiety from fear. Broadly we could say that we feel fear at something specific and anxiety when our disquiet has a less tangible cause. 'Less tangible' might refer to not knowing the size of what might hit us, the likelihood, or the timing. So anxiety is related to uncertainty, but there are other conditions, which are also present, which are to do with ourselves rather than outside factors. They are necessary conditions for anxiety to arise, though not always sufficient in themselves.

One of the most common is boundaries, or more specifically, how we maintain our boundaries. This goes from someone who is not an intimate coming too close (we all have a physical comfort zone, perimeters which we set according to the person we are with, and if someone comes inside our 'perimeter for them', then we feel uncomfortable), through to the prospect of another's demand for our time or attention when we feel unable to say "no" or when what is being asked is inappropriate. For all these situations, the responsibility lies with us. We may not be the encroacher, but now or sometime earlier we have given away our power by allowing our boundaries to become more vague than we can manage. Changing may be something we can do ourselves because we can recognise a pattern like this, but sometimes the start of the pattern may lie deeper and may have involved events or experiences that we could not control. The circumstances have become buried, or the link with our anxiety has been lost. These are situations in which assistance with psychological therapy would be advised. There are also many people who would say that they know themselves as worriers or "the nervous type". A disposition to anxiety of this kind is likely to have its roots in their early years, even from the moment of birth (some would say before birth), and may be part of their personality which will never completely go away. For all of these a diligent practice of mindfulness will be a palliative, though not of itself a cure. An extension of the mindfulness moment may help further. Having achieved a state of non-judgmental awareness of the moment (which will be the more difficult the more anxious you are), reflect on the change you have felt towards a more relaxed state, stay with it for a few extra moments, and tell yourself that you appreciate it. This sort of drawing our own attention to how we feel does not prevent re-occurrence of anxiety, but it will gradually ease the way to reducing its effect.

For some people however, anxiety is all-pervading and hangs like a weight over their very existence. They might know it as agoraphobia or social phobia or generalised anxiety disorder, and with it may come symptoms of panic. Some people know it as a dark shadow and a black negativity about the world. I will call all these existential anxiety. This form of anxiety in the extreme can be paralysing for sufferers because it causes them to withdraw from the world in order to limit their exposure. The withdrawal might be physical, as in agoraphobia or social phobia, or it might be by limiting their range of activity, or it might take the form of an emotional cutting off from engagement with their surroundings, and feeling as if real life was draped in a shadowy curtain which takes away its colour and its vivacity. This form of anxiety accompanies many presentations of depression. With all these responses, which are symptoms of the condition, there is a distancing as an attempt to maintain some sense of being in control. The anxiety is a survival response to the unknown or the unmeasurable.

The ultimate unknown for us all is death, and we unwittingly increase our fear of death by making it an object. In the same way, we make life an object – we more often talk about 'life' than about 'living'. The contribution of the Clear Space Path is in its focus on process, so that life does really become a process of living and not a precious object like a jewel to which we cling. If I had an expensive jewel - which I don't - I might become so afraid of losing it or having it stolen that I would lock it away in a vault. Then I could not enjoy it, even for the time I might have had before it was taken from me. Likewise with life, if I see it as an object, my anxiety arises from my clinging because I might not be able to cling firmly enough. And in the end death will come anyway. Clear Space can offer relief from anxiety-provoking clinging because we cannot cling to processes. We can cling to 'life', if that is how we frame it, but we cannot cling to 'living'. The distancing which is the characteristic of anxiety achieves nothing because it destroys what it is trying to protect. Death will still come – it is the one certainty about living – but it comes as the ending of all processes. In reality death is nothing.

Stress... is insidious. It creeps up on us without our noticing. It does this by reducing our awareness of what is going on, what we are doing. We don't notice that we are working over every night, not just the times we absolutely must; we forget that we haven't taken a proper break; we don't realise that we never say 'no', take on too much, make promises we can't keep without sacrificing our own rest and recuperation time, or help others and end up not being able to help ourselves. The mobile phone, the smartphone, and iPad cease to be tools and become masters.

Stress will eventually produce anxiety and, in common with some anxiety conditions, is almost always to do with boundaries and our failure to set and maintain the boundaries that are appropriate for us at the time. For many there may be aggravating factors – with work stress, competition and/or the organisation's ethic are often factors; for adolescents (and others) peer comparison can be significant; in social settings 'looking good' or 'doing what is expected' is often important. But in all cases the resolution must lie with ourselves. It would not be true to say that we can always set boundaries that alleviate our stress. If we are overstretched by work but, for the survival of our family, we cannot refuse excessive demands and because of the prevailing economic situation cannot find alternative employment, then in the short-term at least we will have to find a way to live with the stress by minimising somehow the toll it is taking on our system.

Stress lowers our immunity, damages our relationships and distorts our reasoning.

Any one of these could produce the event that stops us in our tracks... with a breakdown or cardiovascular illness, through a home life which has become intolerable to our partner, or through a catastrophic mis judgement.

A practice of mindfulness and meditation will not cure stress... and there is a risk. To the extent that such a practice alleviates the symptoms, it may bring a false belief that things are now alright and that no changes need to be made. Thus a re-assessment of one's personal situation and major aspects of one's life is essential. Because of the effect of stress in distorting judgement, it would be important to do this with someone else, at some stage with one's partner, but also perhaps with someone independent and impartial. And alongside such a re-assessment, a regular daily meditation period, if possible at the start of the day, will ease the passage through the day, while short breaks for intentional mindfulness will sustain the steadier emotional state evoked by meditation.

Meditation and Pain...

The way we approach alleviating pain with meditation seems at first paradoxical. Our instinctive response to pain, whether physical or psychological, is to try to resist it in some way. With physical pain this mostly takes the form of tensing ourselves, perhaps tensing our muscles, or perhaps 'freezing' our brain with a mental tension; we will probably swallow hard, and our breathing will stop and start. With psychological pain the resistance will take the form of avoidance, or it may result in self-delusion or fantasising, or it may become displaced into psychosomatic symptoms. All of these come from an instinctive reaction to distance ourselves from what we are experiencing. But the approach of mindfulness is to be aware of the present, to be in the moment with whatever we are experiencing. And so the practice of mindfulness would tell us to turn our awareness towards our pain, minimising the physical or psychological barriers we are putting in the way. This sounds like a leap of faith. It is. But the result is to see the pain for what it is, for physical pain is simply the signal our nervous system is sending to the brain to warn against damage being repeated; and emotional and psychological pain is the expression of the mind's turmoil from unresolved issues.

There is no denying that pain makes concentration difficult in meditation also, when we are trying to reach a clear and open place. It is important when starting your session to pay attention to physical relaxation. When you are steady in your sitting position but with your arms hanging loosely at your sides, turn your attention to your neck and shoulders; notice any tension you feel there, and then in your mind feel your upper arms. Feel them connected to your shoulders, hanging, and with just enough weight to ease out the tension from your neck and across your shoulders. As the tautness in your muscles relaxes, the tension passes harmlessly down through your arms and out of your body. Work through this sequence a few times and, as you do so, become conscious of the weight of your body passing down your spine and being supported by the earth below you. When the tension in your shoulders is relieved, bring your arms and hands to their usual position for your meditation.

Now go into your meditation in the usual way but using the 'breathing that strokes' from the first chapter on meditation. When you reach your clear space, and checking that you are feeling the stroking from your breathing, let your pain, in whatever form it comes, be the part of you that you are sitting alongside. I say "in whatever form", but it is important that it is the pain itself and not its cause which is your other part. If you feel yourself tensing up while you are doing this, come back to your clear space, feel your breathing stroking you and wait for some easing of your tenseness before going again to your pain. While you are sitting, notice any way in which the nature of the pain sensation changes and bring this back to mind when you have finished. Complete your meditation in your usual way.

Using mindfulness and meditation in this way will not make your pain vanish or cure its source. What it can do is help to allow you some separation from the pain itself, some space between you and your pain-tension so that there is more of you available to address the issues which underlie it.

I have also referred to pain in the sections on jealousy and anger. The mindful approach to psychological pain is in essence the same as that towards physical pain. We must approach our pain instead of trying to distance ourselves from it. The most common ways of distancing are denial or projection or depression. If the denial takes the form of getting absorbed in a distracting activity, then there can be a place for this as a temporary measure, as long as it is intentional and with full awareness of the reason. It is also important that it is reviewed in a dispassionate way from time to time.

To project our pain onto another in the various ways we have looked at earlier in this chapter is never appropriate. Respect for our moment, as the principle of mindfulness, implies the respect for others in their moment too. But we can also project onto ourselves, and this is often an aspect of depression. Take as an example a scenario where we suffer injustice or perhaps feel repeatedly taken advantage of in a way which we do not believe we are able to resist. It could arise in work or personal life. It is likely that we will feel angry. Our anger might become aggression towards others who are not connected with the injustice, or it might also be turned inwards. In this way we become the object of our own anger, which starts to carry with it criticism and disdain. In the end we feel diminished, perhaps worthless, and lose our self-esteem. The extreme version of this pattern can be seen with victims of abuse.

In all these and similar instances, approaching our pain draws on the 'not censoring' which was one of our five precepts when we started. It was one of the reasons why it was important to be prepared to take time over the early stages. The mind easily follows a path of self-delusion, and training ourselves to regard the moment without censoring and without judgement is the way we break this. Once we are able to look without censoring and without judging, we are on the way to being self-empathic and being able to feel our anger and our jealousy without censure or rebuke. Now we can allow our pain to be the hurt which we are feeling and replace hostility with sadness, perhaps regret, perhaps resignation, but always a feeling which is immediate and open to consolation as we sit alongside.

7

Clear Space Meditation Path: Part 2

If you followed the first part of the meditation instruction and applied the method as I set it out, you will have gone as far as most people go with mindfulness meditation. If you develop a regular practice of sitting and keep to the five precepts I set out in part one, you will benefit from meditation with a feeling of being more at ease with the world, more able to manage most of the vagaries of life without undue stress or distress, less liable to be stressed or distressed by the actions of others, and less likely to show irritation or frustration. It won't be that your values or opinions or preferences will have changed but that things which used so easily to 'touch a nerve' will now seem to be less of an issue, so that your passage through life will become steadier.

However, there is more in the Clear Space Path. In the introduction I described this approach to meditation as therapeutic. I didn't mean that it was reserved for people who thought they were ill or had some mental health issue. In this context the therapeutic benefit is for us all if we wish to take it up because we are all constantly having to adjust to a world which is changing around us – even our little bit of it – and we are all held back to some degree by our human instinct to hang on to what we know because it feels safer. So, therapeutic in this context might mean the possibility of resolving issues which have been troubling, but it can also mean an open and creative approach to personal development.

This second part concerns this potential for resolution and personal development.

Empathy, the Next Step

To move further along the path, we need to incorporate the concept of empathy. We all know the word, but sometimes coming up with a definition presents some difficulty. The first thing to understand is that 'empathy' is not the same as 'sympathy'. Where sympathy is often about us,[1] empathy is always about another. It is used a lot in writings about counselling and a reasonable definition in this context would be:

> '... the sensing of another person's private world as if it were your own, but without losing touch with your own, without ever losing the 'as if' quality.'

This is close to the definition given by Carl Rogers in one of his papers. It could be visualised as sitting on a seat alongside someone, looking out at their world as they are looking at it and wanting to feel it in the way they are feeling it. It is something we would do intentionally, seeking in some way to reflect our sense of the other's feelings. The result for the person receiving the empathy is the kind of relief and opening up which comes from a reassurance that they are not alone – alone in the sense that it seems as though there is no-one who can, or wants to try to, understand what it is like to be them at that moment.

To use this concept in meditation, we have to modify it slightly. The essential parts of the process of empathy are: intention – it is something we are doing deliberately; a state of interested attention to the other's perspective and feelings; and a putting to one side, but not losing touch with, our own perspective[2]. When we do this in meditation, we are, in a way, empathising with ourselves. By developing the 'sense of something' from our clear space, as in the first part, we are making it possible to go to that aspect of ourselves, when we choose, and empathically 'sit alongside' it. In this way it can stay a 'sense of', without any need to understand it in an overtly reasoning way. The significance of 'sitting alongside' is that we are not looking at this sense of ourselves, rather we are looking out from where we are, as this part. This is important because if we look at something, we usually define it and, in so doing, we fix it as the image we are seeing at that moment. It is fixed because what we see belongs to the moment in which we turned our gaze towards it, and, by fixing it, we are, in a way, preventing it changing, preventing it evolving. But if we sit alongside, with our clear space still available, our 'felt sense' and its presence within us can evolve. Always we can return to our clear space; we never lose the 'as if' quality.

A Meditation 'Conversation'

To give a sense of what this part of a meditation could feel like, I have set out an example below. The left-hand column is written as the meditator might recount his process, as s/he starts the sitting and notices a 'felt sense' arise. The right-hand column is the 'felt sense' itself, arising from an increasing awareness of uneasiness, which comes from the meditator's experience of feeling grounded but then noticing a wondering about whether it can continue. The 'felt sense' starts to be heard as another 'voice' (right-hand column), as I have represented here in dialogue form. We hear fragments of experiences that come from the uneasiness and doubt which the meditator is feeling and knows as part of himself. Alongside these (in the left-hand column) are the reflective (empathic) responses of the meditator, prompting a shift in awareness within the felt sense. And then the return to the clear space.

This is a very abbreviated example of part of a meditation. It suffers from being an attempt to represent in words an internal process, which probably consists not so much in connected thoughts (as it appears here), but in fleeting images, single words and that sense of things which are known and are recognised through un-voiced intuitive responses. It should not be seen as a template or a script, but as one way – by simulating dialogue – to represent how we can extend empathy to ourselves and enable a response from within. In the example a shift happens – the realisation of a possibility of being firmer. In reality such a shift would take longer, or may not happen until a later session, or may happen in the brief contemplation after sitting. Or it may be that one session's 'felt sense' becomes incorporated into something else later in that session or in a subsequent session. It is important that the process is allowed to flow and is not held up by any concern with how it might look. (If you notice that you are thinking about what is happening, then you have probably stopped it happening, so turn to your breathing for a few moments and allow the process to re-establish itself.)

My channel is mindfulness of
breathing; with these three long
breaths I let the tension in my
muscles flow away, and I notice
a spaciness in my arms and my
legs...
my breathing subsiding now to
a natural level, I follow its flow
and I feel its caress throughout
my body...
I am coming to a quieter place,
clear as I approach and free
from thoughts; there are thought
fragments which float through
but they are fragments and do
not remain...
for these few moments the space
within is clear
I feel a grounding... relief...
but now a wondering... how
long?

wavering becoming heady...
and a recognition dimly lit, a
memory... no, a feeling, here
again, creeping in, how long?   Uneasiness when things are
                                     going well, I might not be able
                                     to hold onto it, always like
                                     this...
                                     Always?
                                     Suspicion creeping in...
                                     Spoils things, like when we
I hear your self doubt   thought we understood each
                                     other, my wife, and I'd still got it
                                     wrong, so is it me... I hear what
                                     I want to hear, see what I want
                                     to see?
You don't just let things be ok
                                     I never really enjoy what's there.

                                     Like I'm looking over my
Like nothing can ever be relied   shoulder all the time... but
on   there's nothing there, it's me.

                                     It feels pathetic sometimes, can't
                                     even be happy when things are
                                     good...
And you know it's you doing
it...   And this guy's been around a
                                     long time.
I can sense your sinking feeling
– "oh no, not again, won't I ever
be free of this?"   Yes, that's right, it's about time.
                                     It's about time... hmmm...
                                     That was me with the kids.
                                     Perhaps that's what I need, never

mind giving up, I could be a bit
firmer with myself, like I used to
do with the kids to make them
believe they could do things.

You've done it for them, so you
could do it for yourself...

...

You could rest easier with that?
...   Yes, I think I could.

...

I feel easier with that

...

I rest back with my breathing;
waiting as the space clears;
a feeling of tranquillity and
nothing needed right now

...

When you are ready to extend your meditation practice, add this
in to the additional steps given in the previous part. If you are
aware of a feeling in yourself, separate from your felt sense, as
you work this way; identify that feeling with a word or perhaps
an image or perhaps a colour, so that in your contemplation after
your sitting you can bring it to mind, as a short-hand for your
experience. An explanation of the significance of this feeling in
ourselves when we are being empathic comes next.

The Process of 'Being With'

There is an element in human relating, which occurs across many
seemingly disparate situations. It is the process which I call here
"being with", in the sense of staying with something and simply
allowing our internal response to metamorphose into something
fuller and richer. It starts with the insights into relationship
offered by Martin Buber, when he distinguished the different

ways we use the word 'I'. He differentiated 'I-It' and 'I-Thou'. When we look at a person (or an animal or a thing) and observe or tell ourselves something about it, we imply an 'I', and the other is an object to us. So we might say, "He's got brown hair" and the full version of what we are saying would be, "I see him with his brown hair." In that sentence the 'I' we are using would be an 'I-It'. That's what we do most of the time. But there is another way of being with someone where we don't make the person an object in this way. If we are just with them and don't tell ourselves anything about them, no trying to work them out, no stories, no criticisms, no attitude, just being with them... our unspoken words might be, "I am comfortable here with you," and then the 'I' we have used would be an 'I-Thou'. This 'I-Thou' relationship can offer us a different experience of the other and of ourselves; and it doesn't matter whether the same is happening for them or not.

Let me take what might seem like a rather bizarre example. If right now you look outside and gaze at a tree, or it could be a plant inside the room or a stone, but preferably something natural, initially your gaze rests on an object. If you continue gazing, without in any way trying to describe or differentiate or distinguish or divide, you will find that you see more and more of the tree. You don't need to try to pick anything out; if you stay with it, more and more about it will come to you, and you will start to get a different sense of it. What is happening is that the tree is starting to become 'you and the tree' – a relationship is forming. If you look away and after a few moments look back, that sense will still be there in how you are aware of it. Now recall your sense of the object when you first picked it out to look at, and you will notice a change has taken place in you as a result of your being with it in this way. You might notice this as an ease, which comes from recognition, a familiarity, a smile even.

This is similar to what is happening in meditation when we are sitting with a 'sense of' something in the way I described earlier. Alongside us is our sense of something or someone. But this sense is not anything we can gaze on with our eyes, even though fleeting images may accompany it. It is not concrete like the tree, so no picture can form, though we might describe it as an 'image' in our awareness. As we wait, a feeling forms in response to this awareness and, as we go on waiting, there may be other feelings. So the process of staying with the awareness allows our feeling about it or towards it to come through. This is the first step in the journey of understanding because when we realise and then 'name' our feeling about something, we can make a true response to it in a fully conscious state. And there is more. Because realising and naming a feeling is a step in understanding, it changes the sense itself. It also opens the way for other layers of feeling to arise, which, too, change the sense. All are steps in increasing understanding, altering our awareness, allowing us, in our fully conscious state, to be more real in our responses. This is the therapeutic effect of this meditation path.

Setting this out as I have done, it makes it look as if everything happens in a neat, orderly, even speedy, progression. Of course it doesn't. You may take several sessions sitting beside a sense, which arises consistently, before you notice a feeling come. And then it may be a little indistinct, and it still feels as if nothing really changes. But yet every time a feeling arises and you name it, something changes, however small. You do not have to notice your change in awareness while you are sitting; it may come later, and you may not even spot it at first when it comes. But next time that sense appears in your meditation it will be slightly different, and this opens the way to a new feeling and a new awareness.

It is open to you now, when you feel ready, to take this fully into your meditation. When you are being with a sense of something which has arisen, also listen to the feelings which arise in you in response; name them in some way and hold the memory of them as the sense starts to fade.

You have reached the point at which this meditation path has the potential to be therapeutic in a wider way than simply allowing you to be more relaxed, feel less stress, and be more mindful. It has the potential to affect your way of being in the world, to help you to be more real in your relating and closer to your true self.

Footnotes:

1. At first this seems a very paradoxical statement, but most of us can bring to mind instances where our comforting has in some way been about relieving our own discomfort... we want to feel we are doing something, or we feel awkward if someone is crying, or it is our habit to move into the comforter role. In psychotherapeutic terms there is another consideration, namely that sympathy can often hold the other in their distress and so be disempowering.

2. What is not part of empathy is any reasoning with the other's feelings or rationalising of their situation.

8

A Word about Mantras

Mantras have long been associated with meditation. Mostly they are phrases to be repeated during a sitting to help the mind move to, or be in, the state of altered consciousness which meditation produces. The phrase may have several words or only one, or it may be no more than a sound. All are designed to resonate with the meditator, whether in the mind, or at a physical level, or in a way that links mind and body together. It is important when using mantras that the mantra itself does not become a focus, rather that it is the channel for meditation in the way that I have described using breathing as our main channel in the Clear Space Path. Below I offer some mantras, which fit with this meditation path if they are used in the way I am going to set out. They are generally longer than most mantra phrases, but it is in the way you use them that you will find a resonance.

First bring into your mind the phrase that you have chosen to use. Say the complete phrase to yourself slowly a few times and then repeat the 'words of resonance' to yourself two or three times. The words of resonance are the ones that appear in bold. Now start your meditation in the usual way, and when you feel yourself in your clear space with the rhythm of your breathing alongside you, bring into your mind the words of resonance. They do not need to come exactly as words; rather it is the sense of them that you might seek to touch, as their meanings coalesce in your mind.

It is perfectly alright for this coalescing to come and go during your meditation as your path leads to different places, but each time you return to joining your breathing, bring in the sense of the words of resonance in the same way.

Remember that there is no requirement to use mantras or, if you do find them useful at times, to always use them. In this meditation path they are a facility, which we use if it feels right ... and it could be you find you want to make up your own. Some that I have given may seem to have a resonance for you at specific times or for particular situations, and others may seem more general. That is fine. Use what comes naturally.

Some mantras...

  *being **still, not waiting***
  *sing **softly,** my **soul***
  *letting **go,** letting **free***
  ***becoming** now, **moving** on*
  *gently **being, receiving, giving***
  *being **now** being **here** is **enough***

Being Still, Not Waiting

to be still, without waiting,
to be still, without wanting,
to be still in the quiet beyond the clamour and the hubbub,
in the silence of infinity

The final and greatest challenge for the ego is to be able to be still without waiting, to be still in the moment and be satisfied with the moment. Even simply waiting betrays the ideal of being satisfied with the moment. Even simply waiting begs questions, "waiting for what?" and "what are we wanting?" There is an implication that the waiting would end with the arrival or appearance of something. And even this pulls us away from the present and from being able to be with the present moment and find it sufficient. It is our ego that pulls us away, because it is our ego that does the wanting. In all our wanting there is the inference of being entitled to what we are wanting. That is where we would look for our ego.

A story is told about a traveller, a buddha and a sage...

One day a buddha was sitting by a lake, looking out across the still water. It was a fine day, and there was the gentlest whisper of a breeze, just enough so that the sun didn't feel too hot, just enough to rustle the grass growing at the water's edge, just enough to raise the smell of the warm, baked earth into the air, just enough to carry the faintest tinkle of goat bells from the hills in the distance, just enough for all those things to be with the buddha as he sat by the lake... just enough and no more. As he was sitting, a traveller came along the path and stopped a few paces away. He waited for the buddha to look up and greet him, but the buddha just sat looking out across the lake. After a while the traveller noticed himself becoming irritated and then annoyed and in the end quite angry, until he could contain himself no longer and burst out to the quietly sitting buddha:

"What is this? Here we are, the only two people for miles around, and you haven't even the common courtesy to pass the time of day."

The buddha replied:

"Sit here a while and let the breeze take away your anger. You are angry because you think you are important. But here there is nothing more important than the breeze."

The traveller was puzzled by this answer, but he felt uncomfortable for shouting at the stranger, so he sat and waited, and, little by little they came to him – the sun just warm, the rustling of the grass, a smell of baked earth, goat bells tinkling in the distance. As the sun passed overhead he felt calm and rested and refreshed so that finally he decided he would continue his journey. So he got up and started to walk away from the buddha, who was still sitting. And the buddha said:

"Will you not take your leave?"

The traveller replied:

"There is no-one to take leave."

A little further on, the traveller could see ahead and noticed that his path was soon to be joined by another, and, glancing across to where the other path was approaching, he could see an old man walking steadily in the same direction. He looked wise, like an elder of some ancient faith. A few minutes more and their steps fell together on what had now become one path. This time the traveller felt no irritation or awkwardness as he silently fell in step beside his new companion. In a little while the silence was broken.

"You have come from the buddha," said the sage.

"How do you know that?" asked the traveller.

"Everyone who comes along this path has passed the buddha."

After a few moments the sage spoke again: "What did you learn?"

"I learnt about stillness and about being one with the world."

"And will you hold on to that?"

"I will try."

"And how will your 'one with the world' encounter others?"

The traveller fell silent. Before he had sat with the buddha, he could have answered that, but now nothing from before seemed to fit.

The sage stopped walking and turned towards the lake.

"Look at the lake," he said. "What colour is it?"

"Blue," answered the traveller.

The sage walked on.

"No, the lake is a mountain tarn; it is very deep, and in its depths there is no light. The lake is black; it is the sky which is blue. So does the sky make the lake blue? The sky is just there; it knows nothing of the lake. The lake knows nothing of the sky. But being together they create blue."

As the sage was talking, they had come to where the path became two again. The sage took one, and the traveller knew that he must take the other. After a few steps, the sage looked across to him, raised his hand in farewell and said:

"Being, just being, can be enough."

* * *

Ego is present in all attachments. We address attachments in our meditation when we use the procedure of 'sense of' to facilitate a feeling response to aspects of ourselves both in relation to others and in relation to our own characteristics, in order to bring about a new and growthful awareness.

In the story, the traveller came upon the buddha sitting alone, and, in the way of most walkers in hill country, expects some kind of acknowledgement; after all, you don't meet that many people in these circumstances, so you expect to greet and be greeted. But the traveller was bringing his world into a setting where it did not belong; for him, to be greeted was important because it would mean he had been noticed and his arrival acknowledged as the most important thing in that moment. He didn't stop to take in this new setting. He wasn't mindful. His ego, in that moment his attachment to his need to be noticed, was preventing him being truly present. He was closed off to the possibilities of this world.

The buddha illuminates: the traveller hasn't been noticed and acknowledged and his ego is slighted; he is nobody in particular and this is disagreeable; and so he projects his vulnerability with his petulant remark to the buddha. The buddha outlines the order of importance of things, namely that there isn't an order, and the breeze, which you can't even see, is as important as anything else. So the traveller gives in and waits with the buddha and gradually becomes more mindful. His ego is subdued to the point where, when he eventually leaves, his sense of himself is no more than being a part of the landscape around, and the landscape is always changing. "There is no-one to take leave."

We could look on this first encounter as opening up a path for the traveller. The buddha does almost nothing except offer the traveller a place to be still and open himself to what is around and, in so doing, the traveller discovers himself freed from his ego. The second encounter offers the traveller a vision of his place in that moment. One aspect of being ourselves is allowing ourselves to be. Another is to feel ourselves in relation to what is around us. This idea of relation needs an uncluttered sense of who we are and an undistorted view of the created world around us. And so, in the story, the sage uses the lake and the sky: each can be what it is, but together they create something new, where creature (created object) and creation are together the process, but yet the integrity of each remains. This is the true yin and yang, where black and white, good and bad, form and formless, do not just exist in contrast to each other – they exist because of each other.

And so we have the building blocks of this pathway to freeing ourselves from our ego.

We start with (and we will probably never be completely free from) our ego-bound self, and this manifests through our attachments, which result in our attitudes and make up a large part of how we respond... our attitudes are the outward aspects of our personality;

Because our personality feels like our identity, we become defensive when something threatens our security, and our ego resists change with projection or withdrawal;

Our meditation brings space, the opposite of confrontation;

A 'sense of me and... an aspect of me' can arise, and I can sit alongside this sense and let myself feel;

As feeling comes, resistance softens and attachments loosen, and I can start to see myself as a part of the world around me;

Breathing can be my connection with my part of the world, as I breathe in to receive the world around and breathe out to be present in the world.

There is a risk in setting something out by steps, as I have above – that it appears that the passage will be a short one, that the process will be clear-cut and the stages well-defined, that the way

I have described it will be the way it feels for you. I want to respond to each of these possibilities.

that the passage will be short... it cannot be, because, as human beings, mostly, we change slowly, and there may be a long period of not changing behind us. But more than that, the process of human development ends only with death. We are an integrated whole, which means that when one aspect of us changes, everything connected has to change as well, even if only slightly, and in turn every aspect connected to those connections and so on and on. And something else: as a small boat at sea needs to be constantly balanced to ride waves and wind, so we have to continually be balancing ourselves in order to be comfortable enough on life's ocean.

that the process will be clear-cut and the stages well-defined... it is a truism that nothing in the realm of the psychology of human activity is clear-cut. Our myriad different life experiences ensure that clear-cut definitions linked to predicting outcomes is unrealistic.

that the way I have described it will be the way it feels to you... you start from where you are, and there is no-one quite like you in quite the same place with quite the same view. That is why this path of meditation uses a way for you to touch on your feelings in response to your sense of yourself. (In the terms of Carl Rogers' core conditions, this is being empathic, and also congruent, with yourself.) Here are affliction and relief together, the yin and the yang. Your experience is unique, and your insight too.

* * *

We can all find our own peace. If we cultivate an attitude of mindfulness, peace is relative. So, we may most naturally become aware of peace watching a sunset, or in a sunlit meadow, or sitting on a beach or by a lake with the water just lapping at our feet; but peace can also be a barefoot walk in Hyde Park with the roar of London traffic only a couple of hundred yards away; or lying on the floor of our living room, letting go of the tension in our muscles listening to gentle music; or sinking into the seat after rushing for the bus and now allowing our relief to calm us. Peace is a state of mind. At its heart is being still. And not waiting.

In the summer, when I do my morning meditation by an open window, I often find that I am particularly aware of this 'being still' towards the end, and I notice, while I am still in silence, that I hear a cascade of birdsong close outside the window, like drops of water from an overhanging branch into a still pool, and it will stop, and there is silence again. Then, if I can simply be still, without wondering when the bird is going to sing again, then, I am being still, not waiting. Then I am at peace.

being still, not waiting
being still, not...
being still
being

...

Meditation on the Experience of Peace

I saw the mist slowly spreading up the valley,
gentle touch of water freshening,
sweetness like a damask rose.

Peace is different from stillness; it is different even from silence, though both may be accompaniments.

Peace is a kind of non-interventionist fairy godmother of our being, always just out of sight (because we don't look), but always available if we know how to summon her up, and always on our side. And just occasionally she appears of her own accord.

Peace is an absolute; it brooks no compromise and for each of us can only be an experience from within.

Here is a meditation to cultivate the experience of peace.

Start with three long breaths and allow your out-breaths to smoothe the tensions in your muscles so that you can feel your whole body ease and relax...

Let your breathing subside into a gentle, even rhythm...

Feel yourself moving into your clear space...

Feel the weight of your being, held by the earth, and be aware of this connection...

Let the earth take the weight of your whole being, how it is now and how it has come to this point, and feel the comfort of that support...

Allow yourself a sense of the person you are, in this moment, at this point, which is the end-point so far of the path you have travelled and all that has happened to you...

Move gently between this sense and your feeling of comfort from the earth supporting, grounding you...

Feel the calm of this gentle movement, between the sense of your being at this moment and the feeling of being grounded, and let it resonate in your breathing...

Feel more and more the quiet firmness of the earth's support...

When you are ready, after your usual time of sitting, lengthen your breathing into three long breaths to bring yourself back.

From a therapeutic perspective this meditation is about allowing our story to reconstruct and become the narrative which explains the person who is here now. Peace for each of us can only be the peace of the present, and this can only come with the acknowledgement of our complete person, our whole story.

It is more important than ever, therefore, not to judge anything that appears as we allow ourselves that sense of who we are in the moment, aware that this person contains all the experiences of their life lived to this point. Not judging means not attaching 'good' or 'bad' labels to anything, but simply allowing everything to have been how it was.

You may find it helpful in this meditation to use the "breathing which strokes" and be particularly conscious of the out-breaths (the stroking breaths) each time you return to the feeling of being grounded.

Love and Its Confusions

Rare as the wild pearl
in a crusty oyster shell
unconditional love

Love... parental, perfect, forbidden, unrequited, passionate, puppy, sentimental, obsessive, altruistic... so many notions and descriptions of love to reflect the turmoil it causes us. We probably have more adjectives and expressions for love than for any other emotion. And it's not even just the words themselves. "I love you," depending on tone, speaker, and context, could have at least five distinctly different meanings, of which "I am in love with you" is only one. Ironically, the love in the haiku I have started with – unconditional love – is the meaning we would most often want to be heard by the person to whom we say, "I am in love with you," but it is the meaning least likely to be true. Here is the start of our confusion – the confusion between love and need, which, in the case of romantic love, is most often a confusion of before and after. While I am waiting and agonising, before my love has been reciprocated, I can say in all honesty and good faith, "I would do anything for you." But when I know that my love is returned, I give away a part of my own being to that 'between us', and so "I would do anything" has a condition and becomes "...anything except let you go." My love has created a need because the other person has become part of who I am. Such a paradox!

In order to have faith in the ultimate goodness of humankind when we are beset with so much evidence to the contrary, we create for ourselves an idyll of romantic love as the only aspect of being human which can be pure and perfect and constant, to be an aspiration and a dream. But it can never be so because our very nature gets in the way. The subtext of "I would do anything for you... except let you go," is "My love for you is so perfect that it is all you need, and I am all you need." Taking one view, we might describe these two statements as indicating commitment and self-belief respectively. Taking another, we might say possessiveness and arrogance.

Kierkegaard, the nineteenth century Danish philosopher who wrote about all aspects of human and divine love, implies that perfect love means to love the one through whom one becomes unhappy[1]. Commitment and self-belief bring unhappiness because neither can be one hundred per cent, in the face of the hazards of living; and possessiveness and arrogance, through their very precariousness, create their own despair. So is there no way to avoid this looming pit of despondency?

Perhaps we are asking the wrong question. Let's look at love from the perspective of mindfulness and discover how we represent it to ourselves and how it is present in us.

In the beginning I am a part of my mother. I am born, and then I am physically separated, and so I immediately try to re-connect myself. I orientate myself by touch and smell because that is all that is intelligible to me to begin with. A little later there is sound too, and the world starts to get confusing. Then there is light and colour, and vague shapes appear which start to distract me away from my maternal clinging. And now I want to draw everything to me. My fledgling arm movements try to gather the colourful moving shapes and bring them into my orbit, preferably into my mouth; as soon as I sense my separateness and something attracts me, I try to make it part of me, not for acquisition – I have no concept of that – but for cohabitation. Thus, our instinct for bringing what attracts us into our space and holding onto it if nothing more inviting catches our eye, or abandoning it opportunistically, is more primitive than any feeling of love, assuming, that is, our idea of love is one that contains some giving of ourselves. The infant's 'love' for its mother, at first, is an amalgam of instinctive self-interest (survival) and the residual of a pre-natal connection. So the part of our love which later leads us to say that "my love is perfect and I am all you need" is a combination of infant instinct and, probably, adult delusion.

If you are feeling uncomfortable at this point, it is possibly because you have made a connection in some way with your own experience. It is also likely that this will have led to an attitude, a judgement – perhaps about what I have written, yes, but also about your own feeling. You may be thinking you have been wronged, or you may be feeling guilty; you may be feeling negative about yourself or you may have misgivings. Whatever thoughts are arising from your feeling, let them go and come back to the feeling itself. Try not to search around for what the feeling means, but rather, for now, stay with the sense of what it is. No more. And when you are ready, read on.

In that anecdote about the infant I referred to 'cohabitation' rather than 'acquisition' or 'possession'. As human beings, our most natural response to things that change, other than by our own making, is to try to maintain our sense of who we are. Our referent[2] is always the past because that is what we know, and it has got us to this point. So the infant grasps and gathers to its mouth what it sees because that is what it did with its mother's breast. In later life children will cling on in love because their loved one is a part of themselves, not a possession, but a co-creator of the intimate world in which they exist.

Next to our children, the person with whom we are in love is the 'part of ourselves' we can least afford to lose, "least afford to" because in cohabiting our relationship, they are inhabiting us. Strange words to use, you may think, 'cohabit', 'inhabit', but when we look deep into our sense of "me in my relationship", we find a fabric woven with such a tight weave that we have difficulty distinguishing warp and weft, and the fineness of the cloth means that, were even one thread pulled out, the whole fabric would be irrevocably changed. There is interdependency, and there is also co-creation. To express love like this is not to imply what should or should not be. It is simply mindful observation.

There is another aspect too, which I also refer to in the later chapter "A Sense of a Self", namely that this mindful sense of what our love is does not have to be, in fact cannot be, the same for both partners. So my love is mine, and your love is yours, and what we share is interwoven with the two of us. How does that help? It helps because now I have to take responsibility for my own love. If we listen carefully to the sort of things we say when we've been jilted... "my love is perfect, and I'm all you need", "I've done everything for you", "I've always given you everything you wanted", "I don't deserve to be treated like this"... we can hear in all of these the implication that our loved one is doing wrong. But their love is theirs, and our love is ours, and we each have acted out of our own love as we feel it. The loves that we each feel are not the same. No two loves ever are.

Differences in romantic love cannot be about blame. And they cannot be about deciding right or wrong. They are only about the process. They can lead us to understanding, through mindfulness, through true awareness of all that is present in this moment, without judging. It might seem odd to say that we set ourselves free by taking responsibility. But it is the case, because we can only change how we are ourselves; we can never make other people change. So if we stop demanding that others change, we set ourselves free to do the only thing that is open to us – to change ourselves.

If you are conscious that what I am talking about, love and its confusions, is causing you distress at this moment, it could be a time to sit in meditation with this as the focus, not to try and 'work out' the problem, not to replay old scenarios, not to rehearse a next move, but to use meditation to provide the clear space for a new insight to arise. I suggest the following:

Firstly, if you are unsure about the meaning of what I have written in this chapter so far, then go back and re-read it slowly, and when you are happy you have understood its meaning...

Bring to mind a time when you have felt a real depth of love, unconflicted by doubt or misgiving, and, as you do this, draw yourself in to the feeling itself and whatever sensations arise with it...

As you begin with your breathing to move into meditation, repeat slowly to yourself the mantra...

Letting go, letting loose...

While you are sitting, stay with your feeling of deep love and hold it as a feeling or sensation only – if you find that your thoughts are replaying scenarios, bring the mantra to the fore and hear those words in your mind – letting go, letting loose...

After your normal period of sitting, bring your meditation to a close.

* * *

Sexual love is inextricably linked in our minds with romantic love. But in reality, is it wishful thinking or some knee-jerk assumption which means that we make this automatic connection between sex and love? Certainly throughout history and across the five continents there have been societies (and still are) where the primary function of sex was/is procreation, and love, if it comes, comes later.

In the moment of orgasm we are completely self-absorbed. You might say we are cut off from the world by our ecstasy. Our ecstasy is ours alone, each one of us. Even if we have managed not to neglect our partner in the few moments before, we are on our own for those few seconds of ultimate pleasure. The great 20th century French composer Olivier Messaien, who wrote one of the most remarkable expositions of the winding passage of life, the *Turangalila symphony*, suggested that man comes closest to God in the moment of orgasm. Perhaps... in this sense: that nothing else exists in our universe at that moment – we are all-powerful and totally powerless, and they are the same.

So how to account for romantic love? And how to describe the element, which, added to possessiveness and arrogance and integrating the most self-centred of human behaviours, has the potential to create a bonding that can have a resilience exceeded only by the bond which is the referent for all others: the mother with her child?

The answer lies in that paradox. Being all-powerful, we are powerless. Possessing everything, we possess nothing. In every aspect of human behaviour, once everything has been accomplished, its value disappears. When you possess everything, the very notion of possession is meaningless. If you were all-powerful, then power would be meaningless as a concept. It is as if opposites don't just define each other, but they actually create each other. And so, possessiveness and arrogance, and commitment and self-belief, only exist because their opposites also exist, respectively, generosity and humility and hesitation and self-doubt. All these are constituents of romantic love, in real life if not in dreams. They are complementary in the two-way process of relating. Even hesitation and self-doubt, because these make us people who can receive; unsure of ourselves, there are ways in which we can be helped. In romantic love our weaknesses are our openings. Such relationships are built on the dynamic of mutual giving because there is a willingness to receive, and on mutual receiving because there is a wish to give. So here, in the qualities that bring romantic love closest to a mother's love, we have the possibility of transforming the passion which started out as desire into the emotion which each can call their love, and to let this be the core of the relationship.

Here is the gulf between desiring and loving. Desire is one-sided; it is self-centred, and it is independent of the object of desire – if you say you have no interest in me, it does not affect my desire for you – and we could go further and say that desire always risks blurring boundaries of appropriate behaviour. In fact desire cannot really be called a process; it is an attitude in the sense that I use the word in this book. Loving, on the other hand, is a process. It is the coming together of two loves with one necessary condition – that each is wishing to give, and each is willing to receive. Is it possible to say that this condition is not just necessary but also sufficient? Could that really be true? Nothing to do with sex after all? Well, perhaps we don't need to believe in the necessity of sex – and certainly we would not accept its sufficiency. Desire wanes and the body's needs change. It is nothing to do with individual proclivities, which are, yes, individual, so the activities in relationships will always be different, as the couples we are. No, it is about being mindful of a way of living, which allows two loves to create a mutuality.

In one of my meditations three aspects of loving came to me. They are, if you like, 'subsets' of the description of love we have arrived at here. I offer them to you as possible mantras.

love of kindly watching
love of quietly caring
love of wanting nothing

Footnotes:

1. This is the meaning I take from chapter 2 of "Philosophical Crumbs" – 'The God as Teacher and Saviour'.

2. The base point or value from which other like things are perceived or against which they are assessed.

12

Meditation on Being Alive

Complete stillness is an illusion.

All around us there is movement... sap rising, hearts beating, water flowing, wind blowing.

Every sound we hear has living connected to it... birds singing, neighbours talking, a car being driven, a plane carrying people...

Complete stillness is an illusion.

There are probably 8.7 million species (left) on earth, of which we have catalogued around 1.2 million, of which Man is only one. There is that much living going on. That much turning, beating, oozing, swirling, gliding, floating, swinging, wriggling, curling, rising, falling, sliding, hatching, swaying, galloping, waving, going on... of which we do a tiny fraction.

This meditation is about feeling our place and connecting to that life energy and allowing the movement of all that living to rise in us and draw us in.

Start with three long breaths and allow your out-breaths to smoothe the tensions in your muscles so that you can feel your whole body ease and relax...

Let your breathing subside into a gentle even rhythm...

Feel yourself moving into your clear space...

With your eyes closed, start to notice the sounds around you, the sounds of the outside world coming to you...

Behind every sound there is something living, so go to each

in turn as you notice it and simply be with the sound, without even telling yourself that you like it or that you don't like it, only that there is living there...

Stay close to it for a few moments, not describing its origin, not visualising, but sensing the life that is connected to it...

Now go to another sound, and another...

Sense yourself amongst all this living that you have been touching, alongside it, a part of it, not the centre...

Feel your one-ness with this movement and this life around you and feel it rise in you like a wind surging and uplifting you...

When you are ready, after your usual time of sitting, lengthen your breathing into three long breaths to bring yourself back.

13

A Sense of a Self

In the western world our culture prizes individualism, and so it is not surprising that our psychology spends a great deal of time addressing concepts to do with self. We have a whole host of words and expressions which testify to this – self-concept, self-worth, self-esteem, self-made, self-expression, inner self – there are many others. The result is that we tend to think of the self as a thing, an object almost. The first three of these expressions exemplify this very strongly. If we have a concept of something, assess the worth of something, esteem something, it pre-supposes an object, at least metaphorically, to which we attach qualities and characteristics. So we have, and we seem to need, something which we can evaluate and which relates to how we are and how we feel both about ourselves and about our perfor-mance. More than any other single thing, clients coming to counselling talk about their poor self-esteem. We use self-esteem as a kind of yardstick.

Having a body also traps us in this objectifying thinking process, and we often identify body and self as one object, even though self in its other usages is fundamentally a psychological construct. There is a societal aspect to this too because the experience of most of us in the west is of a society where self-fulfilment (fulfilment of *the* self) is the main driver, and community is ad hoc. (By contrast eastern culture traditionally placed the individual as a component in society first, with sense of self being secondary.)

Here then is the challenge: to understand and practice an approach to living, through mindfulness and meditation, which starts to move away from seeing self as an object ('I-It') in favour of understanding our 'selves' as a 'process being' alongside others ('I-Thou'); and to do this within and despite a culture which reifies ('thingifies') the self. We must spend a little time on this because our progress along the meditation path requires us to experience and contemplate our living in this way, which conflicts, at least superficially, with the culture in which we have grown up, with the way our minds have been moulded, you might say. Since it is practically impossible to depart fundamentally from the culture we grew up in, we need bridges. The sense of space we work with in Clear Space can be one of those bridges and complements a therapeutic experience that fits with our perspective on living.

* * *

If I asked you what comes into your mind when you think of your 'self', you would probably start with some sort of image of your physical self, your body and what you look like, and then I expect your mind would start to wander to what you do and what you like, and then probably you would drift on to your feelings about yourself. Try it, if you like; without starting anywhere in particular, make a list and see what comes up.

I want to take the middle set – what you do and what you like – and loosely categorise these as your potential; and I want to suggest that this is how we might look at the 'self', as potential. So, we have a body, and then there is something else. We have a physical resource, in terms of what our bodies are capable of doing, and alongside that we have our 'activity self', rooted in what goes on in our mind, a mind which is aware of itself (consciousness) and can reflect on itself (reflexivity) and has a will which controls what our body is set to do. What is seen of this self, whether in terms of physical action or social interaction or a combination of the two, is determined by this mind, which contains our dispositions, our learnt responses and our experiences. To some extent these three overlap, but we could look at them individually in this way:

dispositions – pictured actions or responses, which would cause us to say "that is me" or "that's not me"

learnt responses – thinking patterns and behaviours which have come from family, peers, education and the like

experiences – relevant situations which we can look at and relate in a reasoning way to the present situation

All of these together are unique to us as individuals and give us the measure of what is possible for us, our potential, in this moment. We could compare this with the meaning of potential in electricity, where it refers to the difference in electrical charge between two points, and which, when it arises, produces the current, the flow of electricity. If we use this analogy, we could say that our self is always in a situation of being able to respond to a situation (even if the situation is coming from inside), and the response we make is the current. Here the analogy must end because the nature of our response depends on many different variables.

Let me take my own example. When I consider the counsellor-therapist aspect of my self, I might be able to say that I have done a lot of training, read many books, attended seminars, done therapeutic work of my own and much exploration with my fellow professionals, worked with meditation on my own and with others and long followed a path of self-exploration and personal development, but all this is no more than potential, in terms of my being a counsellor, until I meet someone who wants me to accompany them for a while on their journey, as a guide, as a facilitator, as a therapist, or maybe simply as a companion. Until such a meeting, my (therapeutic) self is more or less in limbo. I could apply the same process of reflection to each of the aspects of my self, and I could even go as far as amalgamating them all, at a time when there was nothing going on (no current had been activated), perhaps when I was in my clear space during meditation, and then I could say, "This is me, simply being."

All very well, you may say, but that would mean that there were only two possibilities – a completely passive self or a self that was only stirred into action when something from outside appeared and prompted it. So must we just sit back and wait? It looks that way, doesn't it? But there are other aspects of the self to include.

As we live our lives, especially as we are growing up, but afterwards as well, we interact with others, parents and siblings first, then teachers and friends and peer groups, and we also start to witness the effect of outsiders and society on our life. What we tend not to notice is how each of these interactions makes its contribution to the person we are. It would be tempting to brand some as 'positive' or 'good' and others as 'negative' or 'bad'. But for our purpose here we must resist that temptation because to do so would put a barrier in the way of being able to prize the person we are in this moment. (It would also go against the principle of being non-judgmental, which is so important in mindfulness.) So let us just say that some experiences, if they become a pattern of what we have to deal with, lead us to being more closed and defensive, while others allow us to stay open and fully in touch with the world around us. In terms of how they contribute to our potential, the first is *uncon*structive and the second is *con*structive.

An example might help. I once knew a man who came close to losing his wife and family because he seemed to them not to want them and not to be interested in them. His children avoided him by staying in their rooms, and his wife suspected him of having an affair and became increasingly distant. He felt very alone and unloved, and this made him worse because it seemed as though the only comfort he could find was by turning in on himself. What had actually happened, quite a while before I knew him, was that he had been downgraded at work because of a mistake he had made which had had some particularly serious consequences for his employer. He had told no-one about his downgrading. At home he had done his best to maintain the family's standard of living by taking on extra work in the evening, which he had not told his wife. But still the money became short. And so there were unexplained absences, less money to go round, and he came home very tired. Easy, you might think; just tell his wife because she would care, and she would understand. Certainly she would. But this man had grown up with an older brother who had always been more successful, better at school, went to university and was in a much better job. He had not been constantly reminded by his parents or the brother of this, but that did not prevent him branding himself as second best. And so to lose his first good job in 10 years, the first time he had been able to hold his head high among family and friends, was a calamity. His pattern of not admitting to anything that might allow others to see him as failing was deeply ingrained.

The self puts on masks in many different ways, mostly for protection. The confident person is often unsure underneath; the bully is usually insecure; the unsociable person has likely withdrawn through anxiety. When our mask seems as if it might not be enough, we feel threatened, and we project our fear onto someone else... the confident person becomes self-important and arrogant, the bully lashes out, the unsociable person becomes bitter and blames others. There are less and there are more obvious ways we might use masks, and this aspect of our self comes under the category of what I call 'un-constructive potential'. It is un-constructive because it takes us away from the possibility of being able to simply be, in the sense that the practice of mindfulness requires.

The other not so helpful aspect of the self, which leads to un-constructive potential, is something we have already touched on, namely, attachments and the ego. It is normally suggested that it is the ego that clings on and that attachments are the manifes-tation of the ego. I want to look at it the other way round. That it is our attachments that construct our ego. Attachments are a way we try to avoid being hurt. We cling on to people or attitudes or habits because to let go would push us into unknown territory by creating a gap in the inventory that we know as our identity. We can readily think of examples: having such and such person in my life is part of how I know myself; construing all choices in terms of their greater or lesser material gain has become a part of my character after my early life of relative hardship; regular after-work drinking is something I 'need' in order to maintain my image as a sociable person. I might not be able to let go of any of these or similar habits because they are part of the person I 'need' to be (and it is always less scary to stay with what you know), and so I become the life I am leading. In this way I limit myself. I deny myself choices through being constrained by attachments.

So what about constructive potential, the element that brings with it the possibility that the self as potential can be something other than totally passive or self-destructive? Carl Rogers conceptualises this as the 'actualising tendency', a fundamental part of each of us, which strives to become everything that we can become. He gives vivid pictures of what the effect of the actualising tendency is like – the seaweed on a rock which is beaten down by the incoming tide but then lifts up again when the tide recedes; the weeds which, with apparently flimsy shoots, can push up paving stones. Roberto Assagioli, from a very different stance to Rogers, sees will as being the essential element of the self. As with Rogers, there is a driving force, the self far from passive, but this time imagination, emotions and desire are given a specific role. Perhaps both concepts are necessary, but neither is sufficient in the way we are using the idea of self here. And we have not yet uncovered the source of will.

Without having to bemoan the ever-increasing pace of techno-logical change, which we are so conscious of today, and without having to delve into the finer points of Darwinian theory and evolution, we can readily understand that since the very beginning of his 'developed' existence, Man has always been 'at' something. In any situation in which he repeatedly finds himself, he tries to work out a better way to achieve what he wants. Generally this means a way to achieve the same outcome faster, or with less effort, or a better outcome without any more time or effort, or if possible, a combination of all of those. This is different from all other species. At its core is our unique ability to concep-tualise. We don't just see something as 'activity', we see it as 'outcome + *our* activity'. It means that we are free to vary each, as well as observe the nature of the relationship between our activity and outcome. From this comes the possibility of choice, not just between one existing thing and another but between something that exists and something which might be able to exist, or even between two things which both might be able to exist.

So does this account for will? Almost. There is one other respect in which Man is different from other species: we are able not only to know what we feel (with many species we share the experience of feeling pain and other physical sensations, and with the higher mammals we share the ability to experience emotions, such as sadness and happiness), but also to know *that* we are feeling. That bit is called reflexivity. It is these two together – conceptualising and reflexivity – which account for our being able not only to choose something but also to apply our will to it, or in other words to intentionally channel our energy towards it. Peeling away the layers in this way, we can under-stand how both Rogers' 'actualising tendency' and Assagioli's 'will' fit together to contribute to an idea of self which can be consistent with a meditation path that reduces attachments and diminishes the hold of the ego. The ability to conceptualise a possible different present, and the possibility of being able to place ourselves into it in our mind, because we have consciousness and can reflexively know what we are feeling, means that we make a choice for what is more in the interests of our well-being, and we form the intention to apply our energy in that direction. This is our self acting, and it is unique to each of us because our dispositions and our memory (of our past experi-ences) are unique and come into play in both our conceptualising and our reflexivity.

Now we have a model of the self, which we can fit into the way our meditation path focuses on process. It allows us to hold onto the notion of a self of some substance, which is so embedded in our western culture and so necessary for our everyday living, whilst also achieving the mindfulness of meditation, where the self is no more than the moment to moment experiencing of the immediate present. In summary:

Self is potential...

potential consists in constantly having available the possi-bility of increasing well-being through will;

will uses consciousness and reflexivity and instinctive choice of life over death, better over worse, to transform each moment into the next;

each self is unique because the memories and dispositions (which enter into consciousness and reflexivity) of each of us are always unique.

There is a continuity in the self, when viewed in this way, which otherwise seems to be lacking when we are thinking of mindfulness being a focus on each moment as a slice in time. Dispositions we have mentioned, and we might link these in to genetics and inherited traits, but they also evolve with our learning through our experiences. However, the action of our will, through consciousness, is always referencing our memories, while our reflexivity is giving feedback by making us aware of our emotional responding. Moment to moment there is a 'drawing in' of how we were in previous moments and previous times. The contribution of our self from earlier times gradually becomes diluted but never completely lost, because, even if we have forgotten a particular incident which caused a change, its effect is contained in what our will draws in to take us forward.

To release the self from the bondage of being an object opens up the full potential of a meditation path which can be truly therapeutic. In a sense, the self as process gives us our cake and allows us to eat it. Not being held as an object by our 'I-It' stance, it is freed to flow because our view from 'I-Thou' means that we can no longer imprison it with snapshot perceptions. It – we – can act from the combined potential of who we are and each presenting moment.

14

Meditation on Being Just Who I Am

don't burden memory with expectations,
just let it be what has been

We have lived these many years, and we must value all that they have brought.

We have trodden so many roads yet still could feel the buzz of starting here.

We have met so many others who have shaped the one we are, and all should have a place because of who we are and because we must respect the one we are, prizing our story for all its many parts.

We cannot love others unless we love ourselves, and we cannot love ourselves unless we love this person here and now... with all our many parts, and for everything we are.

Here is a meditation which helps to integrate a true sense of the person you are.

Start with three long breaths and allow your out-breaths to smoothe the tensions in your muscles so that you can feel your whole body ease and relax...

Let your breathing subside into a gentle even rhythm as you move into your clear space...

When you are at ease in your clear space, turn your attention onto yourself but don't look inward; rather feel your whole self, sitting as your are...

Allow a sense to develop of being both the observer and the observed, seeing and being seen almost in the same instant...

Notice without judgment the different parts of you, both what is visible on the outside and what only you know on the inside, and treat everything that comes into your mind equally, nothing is good and nothing is bad, but here everything is simply a part...

As you notice more and more parts of you, aspects of your life, people you know past and present, each with a place in your story, be aware of the sense of you and these parts and let them all form into a thread which comes through your life to this moment now...

Let your sense of the thread, your life, you as the observer and the observed, and where you are now, all merge into one...

Look for a feeling of ease within yourself and turn your focus to it...

When you are ready, after your usual time of sitting, lengthen your breathing into three long breaths to bring yourself back.

15

Clear Space

We need to fill out a picture of how this clear space, which is a reference point for our meditation path, might actually be felt. So far I have let it have a simple spatial context, with metaphors which allude to open fields or expanses of water or the clear sky, but these are metaphors, and in the end we must get closer to the pure experience. Straightaway, though, we encounter difficulties because language, which is a means of concretising the phenomena of our world in order to convey our view to another, copes only partially with those phenomena which cannot be made into objects. In terms of Buber's 'I and Thou', language is always in the stance of 'I-It' in relation to what it is representing. For this reason, it depicts all it describes as static, even if the objects in its narrative are themselves in motion. So, we might say, "I have been quite down, but now it is starting to lift." and we would be describing a process that has been happening and is therefore something which in this moment is in the past, rather than a feeling going on as we are talking. If we were to attempt the latter, it could sound something like, "easing, lighter, seeing further now ahh gentle softening", which would probably be nearer our actual experience in the now, though not very grammatical.

Our attempt to represent Clear Space presents us with similar difficulties.

If nothing else, though, we can be clear that Clear Space is not a void, so our difficulties will be with how we describe what is around in it, which makes it different from 'void'. To begin with, we can see it as the 'ground' on which other things happen or appear. In this sense it is a facility, something which is there and can be returned to, hence the spatial metaphors of previous chapters because we tend to think in terms of returning to places. But the idea of 'ground' adds to this more than just spatially. I use the word here in the sense in which it is used in Gestalt therapy. In that approach, 'ground' signifies a state of quiet abiding, an equilibrium in the moment, within which a wish or need or impulse arises and moves into awareness with an increasingly acute insistence until it is satisfied and we return to a new equilibrium in a state of rest. Using this paradigm, psychological un-wellness comes from interruption, by suspension or blocking, of this process of satisfaction. Applying a similar concept to our meditation, we can say that the processes which happen in and around the ground of our clear space can be what they are and, in not being blocked, are validated as what they are by our returning to this ground.

In the chapter "A Sense of a Self" I used the idea of 'potential' and suggested that we can conceptualise our Self as potential. We can carry the same notion across to Clear Space. At any time when there is nothing going on in our being, or at least nothing that comes into our awareness, there is nevertheless the possibility of something starting to arise. That something may come from inside us or it may be a stimulus from outside. It may be very little and need us to check to make sure that it is really there, or it may be something more substantial and perhaps intrusive. But sooner or later, something arises, from our inner world or from our outer world, and it is this certainty for which we use the term 'potential'. The certainty comes from the fact that all things are constantly changing, are constantly in that process of becoming even slightly different from what they were. We too are part of that process, and it affects us in a particular way because of our dual consciousness, that is, because we can both be aware and also know that we are aware.

Our picture so far, then, is of Clear Space as the 'ground' around which is the potential offered by our internal world and our external world. These worlds we carry around with us all the time, and moment to moment they create the potential which is our Self. They each have different layers. Our internal world at its deepest level is the source of our emotions – the word emotion itself means a 'moving out' and so can be seen as the manifestation of our most profound awareness of ourselves in the moment. Because this awareness comes from deep, it changes slowly. Less deep, and so more volatile, are our feelings, which may match but may also appear at variance from time to time with deeper emotions. So, we might know ourselves as carrying sadness because of a loss, and this is like a weight which is always with us, yet we can still smile and reflect the happiness of children at play. The sadness hasn't gone away, but we also feel some of the happiness of the children.

Then there is a layer which contains the sensations which our body gives us, whether those are momentary or lasting, whether imposed by condition or illness or some physical constraint, or whether they are part of our bodily functioning like eating or breathing.

And so we come to our thoughts, which may be stimulated by emotions or feelings or sensations, but also by observation of our external world. We could say that our thoughts are tri-polar. They have a referent in a stimulus internally or externally; they have an interpreter in the form of memory (whether that is of an event that has happened or of a way we have found to understand something and in which our reasoning plays a part); and they have a process, which I have already referred to as replaying or rehearsing or imagining, but they can also be reflecting our present awareness.

Such is our internal world... and it is constantly changing. Our external world too is constantly changing, partly through our interaction with it and partly because it is composed of more than just us. It too has layers, related to its immediacy for us. So, a task which we are engaged in and which requires intense concentration commands our highest level of attention, while our expectancy about going out tonight is more of a floating awareness, and our general sense of ourselves and the way we manage our life is no more than a programme running in the background.

These worlds, then, create the potential which is present in our clear space. From time to time – all the time outside meditation but also within our sittings – the potential ceases to be potential and becomes movement, a current flowing. But when there is no current, just potential, there is stillness, held between now and the next moving, marked by the passing of our breath.

It is to the quality of our breathing that we must turn briefly, not so much the pattern of our breathing (the different modes of breathing that I referred to in the third chapter) as the sense of what our breath is for our body and our being. Many people do not give their breath or their breathing a second thought – it is simply something that goes on working. Many people have very shallow or uneven or laboured breathing and are unaware of it. But our breathing is both affected by and affects us, and so it is important in our meditation. When meditating we want to clear a space for parts of us which are normally submerged or obstructed to take their place in our whole person, and so it is important that we feel a good relation to this marker of our process, our breathing. I liken this relation to that between the swell and the ocean. Wherever you are on the ocean, there is a swell. If we are the ocean itself, we cannot be without our swell. If we are the rising and falling motion of the swell, we only exist in the vast volumes of the ocean. This is the sense of ourselves and our breathing. Experiment now with these images. Spend some time interweaving a picture of the ocean swell, with its gentle undulating motion, and your breathing, with its steady rise and fall. (But take care if you are liable to sea-sickness!)

When we have started to reach that unity between being and breathing and to feel the tranquillity of our clear space, we yet encounter an aspect of this 'being in mind' which can draw us away into unintentional cognitive process. In day to day language we would probably say our attention wanders, but if we delve a little deeper we can inform our practice.

There are two aspects to the process of being in mind: one is resting and the other is attending. They are a version of yin and yang because they are each part of the other and still are opposites. If, as you are sitting here now, you think relax – just that, no tensing and releasing of muscles, no working through the parts of your body, just think relax – you will find that you achieve a release which you can feel physically in some way, perhaps a sort of vague fuzziness in parts of your body. When you feel it, just let it be. It can be warming and comforting. Before long you will lose it. Your mind-body will have found something else. It is as if we cannot rest, and if nothing grabs our attention from inside or out, then we will go searching. And searching always brings in our reasoning side. So, from thinking, we have created a relaxed state, and then that resting itself has set off attending in the form of searching. This seems to be a part of the human condition, lessening as you get more experienced with meditation but never completely absent. We cannot banish it. We must accommodate it, if we want to progress. Try that exercise again, but this time, when you feel that relaxed sensation, intentionally notice it (but without thinking anything about it), and then in cycles of between 2 and 20 seconds keep intentionally noticing it. (I stress that the noticing should be almost visceral, only minimally cognitive.) You will find that you will be able to stay with this relaxed state longer and longer.

Whether or not you use this relaxation as part of your channel into your clear space – and I suggest that you experiment with combining 'think-relax' with your breathing to find what works best for you – this loop of visceral noticing will help you maintain the clear space which you create. It will not hinder the sort of movement or arising of awareness from a 'felt sense' which becomes material for our meditation, but it will keep clear the space itself for this to happen.

It often seems like an irony of human process that more significant things happen when we are not trying. In reality there is no irony because it is part of human process itself.

Our reasoning side is all about meaning. In all we encounter we seek to discover meaning. We associate understanding with the discovery of meaning. And in understanding we place ourselves in an 'I-It' stance with the object of our attention. Our emotional side, on the other hand, is all about experiencing. In each moment, if we allow ourselves to be open, we are able to flow with the stream of our experiencing, whether it originates from our internal world or our external world or a combination of the two. In open experiencing we place ourselves in an 'I-Thou' relationship with its source. But open experiencing often seems more risky than reasoning, and the more open, the more risky. Still, we must go there because the movements which become significant steps in meditation do not arise from reasoning.

It is true that, when something arises which we follow because it resonates with where we are at that moment, our reasoning side is involved. We cannot have a single thought without that being the case. But, before the thinking is the arising from the ground of our clear space. The arising comes from deeper down and is akin to a sense of something which has its origins somewhere in our body, without any intentional cognitive intervention. When it comes, it seems to be from somewhere just beyond our edge of awareness, and the first cognitive intervention, which is unmediated, is to attach a name to it because that is what our reasoning does. If we name, if we label, we feel safer, because in a small way, we know the 'size' of a thing. (Like when you have a nagging pain which doesn't feel like anything in particular but seems to instill in you a kind of foreboding; if you go to the doctor and find that your pain is recognised and has a name, you feel some relief.) In a similar way our reasoning grasps at our 'felt sense', names it, defines it and in so doing gives it boundaries. If we let that be an end to it, then our reasoning side will have closed down the channel from which the movement is arising. So in our clear space we must stay available at this edge of awareness so that our reasoning can be continually updated. Paradoxically, a means of doing this calls on reasoning itself. (Not everything about naming is limiting to our process in meditation.) When a 'felt sense' arises, it is also useful to name it but then to 'shuttle' between this name and the sense itself. We will be looking for anything else about the sense, which is not completely caught in the name. This way the process stays open and fresh.

Here is a summary of the points so far in this chapter:

- our clear space can be seen as a stillness 'held' by potential
- the stillness itself and the possibility of movement from our internal or external worlds create the potential
- new awarenesses can arise from our internal world, which has the different layers of emotion, feeling, sensation and thought, and they can arise from our external world with its different layers related to the immediacy of their significance to us moment by moment
- a right relation to our breathing allows this to be a marker of our clear space
- we can hold our clear space by regularly noticing its presence
- in our clear space we can notice a 'felt sense' arise from our edge of awareness and name it and still be open to other movements at our edge of awareness

* * *

I have talked already about 'felt sense' and empathy being our response to it as we sit alongside. It is time to re-visit this aspect of our meditation, if you have started to work in this way in your sittings.

Everywhere that I talk about 'felt sense' I have bound 'me' into the 'felt sense'. I have always understood it as a "sense of me and ..." So whether the other in the 'felt sense' is a person, or a part of my life, or an aspect of my character, or the feeling that comes when I think about a particular thing, or no more than the mood I am in in this sitting, I am always in there as well. The 'I' in that last sentence was the origin of the 'felt sense', and the 'felt sense' arose from within the 'I'. The 'felt sense' never becomes completely separated. The relation is always one of 'I-Thou'.

I have already given an example in the chapter "Clear Space Meditation Path : Part 2" of how a 'dialogue' between the meditator and her 'felt sense' might sound – as far as it is possible to represent a process which will usually not have coherent thought threads attached to it and where the voices on either side of the 'conversation' might often seem simultaneous. It could be useful now to look at an example of three consecutive sittings, in which a 'felt sense' appears and moves in the first sitting. Some aspects of the following sittings then seem to resonate with it. In offering this example, I must stress again that it is not a formula or a template. It appears here in order to illustrate how the seemingly disparate material and processes which occur in a sitting can be steps which lead the meditator to greater self-awareness and understanding. The material is real, and the account is of three consecutive daily sittings of the meditator (M), (M is a man), interspersed with my comments for clarification, which appear in right-justified italics. Each sitting was close to 30 minutes.

Sitting I

M begins this and all his sittings with lengthened breaths accompanied by 'think-relax' as he allows his breathing to subside. As he begins each sitting he wonders how he will feel himself settle, aware that sometimes there seems to be "a lot going on" and his mind seems "hyper", which gives him a very physical sensation of being taut as he moves towards his clear space. This can then put up an invisible barrier which holds him at a distance from his clear space. He feels this a little, coming to this session, so to help he gives himself a sense of resting on his breathing, almost that his breathing is a bench he comes to sit on which transmutes to a sensation of his body grounded. The ground where he is sitting slowly becomes clear space.

Breathing, metaphor and physical sensation can be a method of centring ourselves.

M starts to feel comfortable and steady with only wisps of thought intrusion. Then his initial tautness seems to be hovering once more, and he starts to feel helpless. It is a little while before breathing comes back into his mind, and he goes back to breathing as a bench to sit on, and slowly the space becomes clear and still again.

We must be gentle with ourselves, even when it seems we have 'failed' so quickly; failure becomes an attitude, and we are seeking to be without attitude and simply accepting.

Tautness is still around, but now it is slightly outside, like something he can look at and not feel it might take him over. It is not uncomfortable, and he allows it to stay there, away from him, though still in his awareness. Dimly M senses a parallel process to the tautness, inside but undefined. He shifts a little and wonders about pride... no, hurt pride; it isn't completely comfortable. Is this where the tautness was coming from? He realises he is questioning and wants to leave "hurt pride" in the space and wait. There is no context. Might there be? Now he is trying for something and shouldn't. But trying. Suddenly trying and hurt pride go together, and he has a different feeling which seems to be to do with being a trier who is turned down and is hurt.

The cognitive (reasoning) sense of trying for something is not what the 'felt sense' is pointing to; rather the act of trying, and in this way the 'felt sense', leads away from the immediate to something broader.

M said that he started to feel a slight separation between himself as a person who was a trier and where he was at that moment, sitting with that other sense of himself in his mind. Following his training he wasn't letting stories and examples get in the way but let those float away much like idle thoughts. He stayed with this sense of himself as the trier and realised that he was feeling quite sad.

His sadness was the empathic feeling in response to the trier.

M stayed with this 'tableau' for a while as his sadness increased. He started to have a sense of his sadness as something which was lying all around him but then began to become more aware of his breathing. It felt steady and reliable, and he was aware of feeling that it was holding him. A thought came: "OK." The tone was resigned satisfaction. M took time ending his meditation by re-experiencing clear space and noticing over and over his grounded feeling.

The experience of watching the mind watching is similar to the Buddhist notion of "sheshin", and staying open allows us also to notice our own empathic response.

Sitting 2

M realised that this morning he was looking for some kind of solace from his sitting. Having been touched by his own empathy, particularly coming out of the sitting the previous morning, he saw that he was wanting to carry forward what felt like a reassuring theme. His mindful awareness before the session was of the comforting feelings these observations evoked. M paused before starting and was then able to identify another layer of mindful awareness, which was the escapism which his mind was involved in by focusing on the comfortable feelings.

Now M began his initial breathing and think-relax as his

channel towards his clear space.

Becoming calm and still happened quite easily. He was able to notice his calmness, and for a while he did this and then noticed that he stopped noticing. Now he just waited. M said that a memory appeared in a way that they sometimes do, without any apparent link to his very immediate and sensation-focused state. On this occasion the memory was simply the word "escape", which he related to his secondary awareness before he started this meditation. He tried to treat "escape" as a thought and allow it to float away, but it persisted, and so he let his attention to stay with it.

My belief is that M was testing, and, when "escape" remained, he could treat it as a genuine present thought which might be connected with a 'felt sense'.

M looked for anything connected with "escape" that he could find in his body. Two associations appeared: relief and an empty sensation in his stomach. But he did not think that was all.

"Relief" might have been more cognitive while the feeling in the stomach was visceral, so the possibility that the 'felt sense' contained both but was also something else.

M noticed after a while that he had become distracted and his mind was following idle thoughts. He brought himself back to clear space by experiencing his breathing as more deliberate and located in his physical being, which he could feel being supported by the ground beneath him.

M was aware that there was something which was almost present but not completely in awareness, and he was also conscious that it did not match either the relief from before or the stomach feeling. He waited and knew that he was starting to feel restless. Then it was the restlessness which seemed to be the 'felt sense'. He shuttled between the word and the feeling to test it, and "unfinished" came up.

M said that he then experienced a wave of emotion and a flood of images, which went back many years and came from work, social and family settings. Loosely they related to activities or situations that he had walked away from. They presented as a kind of chronicle, and his sense was increasingly that of being accused. He felt increasingly uncomfortable and turned to his breathing as a kind of defence against this. He described, as he was beginning to feel steadier, hearing a disconsolate version of his voice saying, "Sometimes when I look back over the years past, it looks like a hostile land." Then, from somewhere inside him, came the sense of a response, but without specific words – now / passed on / not always.

A dialogue between the sense of a part of us and ourselves as the empathic observer can have different appearances and be of varying length. Here it is no more than a single 'exchange' and has no particular metaphoric setting.

M said that once again he ended his sitting with a fairly long period of "just sitting", alternately noticing thoughts and noticing his own sitting.

It was his custom to give himself a few moments of contemplation after his sitting to bring to the fore his appreciation. This time he recalls that some occasions came into his mind when he had been loyal to those around him.

It is usually not useful to attempt to connect up strands from a meditation – to do this would be to make meditation into a therapy and lose its value as a companion. It can be helpful to carry over awarenesses from meditation into a therapy, whether that is an activity with a therapist or a form of self-counselling, but in either case it predicates a process which intentionally calls on reasoning as well as awareness and insight.

Sitting 3

M had been reflecting on the previous morning's meditation and had decided to read through and perhaps incorporate the themed meditation "being just who I am" into this morning's sitting. He read it right through, being open to one part or another finding a particular resonance with how he was feeling, which was composed and methodical. The theme he picked out was that of opposites – observer/observed and inside/outside. He contemplated for a few moments the notion of opposites being together in the same space and the paradoxical sense of togetherness and separateness being in relation.

M described the start of his meditation as particularly placid. He had a picture of his breathing being perfectly flat, like the surface of a lake with not a breath of wind. This morning his clear space had an image which contained a lake and open green grassland and drifting white fluffy clouds. He noticed himself looking at this image and then noticed his slight scornfulness at the cosy feeling within him that it seemed to pander to.

M related that throughout this sitting there had not seemed to be any consistent theme. He had more than his usual thought intrusion but that they were of a very "light" variety, and always, in the background, was the undisturbed lake which was the simile for his breathing. The thoughts that came seemed to be there and not there at the same time.

At one point M noticed a slight impatience which he was feeling and wondered if this was because "nothing was happening". Then he found himself trying to manufacture process by returning to the notion of opposites being in relation. This led to rather intellectual and philosophical reasoning, which felt engaging and sterile at the same time.

Finally M found that what genuinely resonated with how he was in this sitting was to let himself be as he was. With this came a calm which was at one with the calm of the undisturbed lake.

In his contemplation after the sitting he was able to be thankful for both the repose which he had finally found and the wandering process of arriving there. As an aside he mentioned that he had wondered whether it was his ego which had interfered in the form of wanting him to "make something of" the sitting. He thought that he might look at that again.

*Here was an example of a sitting which we could read as following
the thread of the previous sessions, but in a very oblique way… or
perhaps there was no connection to be found at all. It still served as
companion, and we might say, a very caring companion, in allowing a
respite from the fairly heavy emotional process of the previous sittings.*

* * *

It is important to remember that meditation, whilst its effects
may be therapeutic, is not a therapy. The example of M, though
only a small sample, shows that a meditation practice is not best
viewed as a method for problem-solving. Though it can offer
insights, it only rarely offers clear-cut conclusions or neat
arguments. So meditation is not so much the map for your
journey as your company along the way. But that role should not
be undervalued. Our lives are often lonely habitations, whoever
we might be sharing our dwelling with. So a companion, which
can be consoler, inspiration, empathic listener, friendly cajoler, or
simply a comfortable place to sit and wait, is also a good friend.

Many approaches talk in terms of enlightenment through
meditation as a progression through stages of awareness or
higher states of consciousness. Whilst these are not intended as
tests, to many they will be felt that way, and so I would offer an
alternate paradigm.

Meditation can be your companion, but it cannot be the
pathway.

Rather than thinking about goals or end-points, whether we
would see them as enlightenment or heaven or nirvana, we can
look at our passage through life as offering continuing possibilities of harmony between our internal world and our external
world. Our external world is constantly changing, and a practice
of mindfulness and meditation can be the means of staying in
tune and maintaining the modulating harmony between
ourselves and a living, changing world around.

16

Meditation of Benevolence for our World

In giving we receive.
In helping we are helped.
With goodwill we heal, not just others but ourselves.

It is a natural extension of our meditation theme of being alive as a part of the community of all things living, that we should wish well (benevolence) for all people and everything living. If it falls to us to be able to actively help alleviate the difficulties of others (beneficence), then we are more fortunate still. But the process of simply wishing well, in the context of a meditation of benevolence, can also have a practical outcome because in wishing well for others, we acknowledge their humanity. If we can do this for people we do not know and cannot see, how much more is possible for those with whom we are in contact. Then we can see our own humanity, not as the centre of our individual world, but as a part of a world we are sharing.

Here is a meditation on this theme:

Start with three long breaths and allow your out-breaths to smoothe the tensions in your muscles so that you can feel your whole body ease and relax...

Let your breathing subside into a gentle even rhythm...

Feel yourself moving into your clear space...

Centre your attention on your body and how it feels to be supported by the earth below you, allowing you to feel your presence as a being in the world...

Let this become your 'felt sense' of yourself at this moment and name the comfortable feelings that start to arise in you...

As you name each comfortable feeling, bring a person to mind that you would like to be feeling this same thing at this moment...

Continue to go round and round each feeling in turn, each time naming a new person that you would like to be feeling it...

As you continue to cycle round the feelings, individual names can become less important as you extend your benevolence to a wider and wider circle of people and then groups of people beyond your acquaintance...

When you are ready, after your usual time of sitting, lengthen your breathing into three long breaths to bring yourself back.

17

On from Here...

Be kinder than necessary,
for everyone you meet is fighting some kind of battle.
J.M. Barrie

I have often been asked, "Where is the moral dimension in all this?" It is a question that I myself frequently asked in relation to the person-centred approach, which was my first avenue into psychological therapy and is still the bedrock of how I work. The same question could be asked of any of the therapeutic models. Having set out the Clear Space Path and having written what I have here, especially the chapter "A Sense of a Self", I am still very aware that there is nothing in any of the theory or the practice that I have set out myself which says, "This is what is moral and good; this is right and that is wrong." I have re-formulated our self as a set of processes drawing on our dispositions and our memories and on instinctive human nature, which always chooses the more over the less advantageous, and, in that aspect in particular, is orientated predominantly towards self-interest.

Yet there is goodwill between human beings. People help each other; people care about each other; people give without needing to be thanked; people do seek to be sensitive to how their neighbour sees the world.

So where does it come from, this current of human kindliness? Do we have to believe in God? No, I don't think so. A faith in an external source of moral guidance may be the most efficacious and most fulfilling for many, but I do not believe it is a necessity. How then to determine 'what I should do', given a free choice?

I do believe in 'good'. But I also believe that our ability to determine what is 'right' as opposed to 'wrong' in any given situation, individual or societal, is much more limited than we understand. And so I believe in human kindliness.

A story is told of Sadam Hussein, cruel despot that he was, that, whenever he was in the area where he was born and was driving past the farm in which as a boy he was abusively made to live and sleep in a hovel, he went quiet and turned away.

Nothing is ever just one thing.

"Be kinder than necessary, for everyone you meet is fighting some kind of battle."

I have avoided framing a view of meditation as a path towards a dissolution of the self. When we have talked about 'clear space' it has always been *our* clear space. We are always conscious of an 'I' and the insights of Martin Buber offer us a richer sense of the way we feel and express ourselves as 'I'. In defining the 'I-Thou', he identified how we are able to be with another in relationship without limiting it and without it limiting us. In line with this, the 'being in the moment' of our mindfulness allows action, not just reaction. The potential, which we talked about in relation to self, manifests as a choice, which we make in each moment, about how we are going to act. But is our choice always and ultimately in our own self-interest (as the advocates of 'kin selection' claim), or group affiliation (as Edward Wilson, another eminent biologist, argues), or might it be mediated by some other factor? Fortunately, our purpose in proffering theories is slightly different in the psychotherapeutic, as opposed to the biological, field. Here, we have to work with explanations which provide a best fit (because scientific proof involving matters of the mind is rarely available to us), and our main concern is to offer algorithms for a better future rather than provide a mathematical derivation of the present. Our emphasis is less on how something has come to be what it is, as on what it could be after this.

It is my observation, from teaching and practising mindfulness and the Clear Space Meditation Path, and from using both alongside 'conventional' and creative counselling work, that a gradual shift away from awareness of self as an object towards a consciousness of our own process moves us away from self-centredness and towards encountering all others as equivalent to ourselves and their world views as being as valid as our own. Alongside this, it appears that the practice of empathy towards ourselves – the sitting alongside a sense of ourselves – is also good training for an empathic way of being towards others. Here then, within these two processes, I believe we find the source of our beneficence. It is already present naturally in all of us to a varying degree without training in mindfulness and meditation, but it seems to be enhanced by a practice of this meditation path.

So where does this go now and how do you continue along the path?

The first step was mindfulness, and that is always the central core of our practice. It is both bedrock and refuge. In the words of the sage in the story: sometimes just being can be enough. And sometimes just being is all that we can manage. But the practice of mindfulness is a dynamic one. Nothing stays just as it is, and so your evolving acquaintance and familiarity with mindfulness leads towards the Clear Space Path. Mindfulness and meditation need not be felt as two separate things, but rather as aspects of each other. Clear Space opens up your mind to itself. It invites the 'sitting alongside', which is the next part of your journey, and deepens self-understanding by bringing acceptance through empathy. Empathy has no attitude and no agenda; it does not approve or disapprove but allows what has been to have been and what is now to be just what it is now. The effect of working in your clear space is to bring in the world around you with a new immediacy so that what develops is a process of co-creation, of yin and yang, because the bringing in of the world is also a reaching out to the world. From this comes the possibility of your practice incorporating the beneficence towards others, which is the dynamic and outward manifestation of the internal path.

It would be tempting to visualise this, partly because of my metaphor of 'path' as a progression to an end-point. But this path, like all good paths, meanders. Like a mountain path, it has bends and twists and often looks back, and sometimes we think it might meet itself again... but it never quite does. So it's alright to pause along the way, to take refuge for a while in what we know, before moving on. Always we can revive ourselves in the same way as we began...

with stillness in mind

Appendix

Buber, Rogers and Gendlin

Martin (Mordechai) Buber was born in Vienna in 1878 and died in Jerusalem in 1965. He was an Hasidic Jew, a movement within Judaism which sees every aspect of life as integrated with one's faith in God. He also advocated a Jewish-Arab state, without domination of Arab by Jew, and as a common homeland, rather than the independent Jewish homeland, which was the aim of most Zionists. He is best known for his seminal work, already referred to, *I and Thou*, which he wrote in German in 1923 and was first translated into English in 1925. It set out the dialogic basis of his philosophy, which centred around his belief that Man was only truly human when in relation. His language is often idiosyncratic and poetic and the translation by Ronald Smith (the first translation) is the one I would recommend, even though it is the more difficult, feeling, as it does at times, a little like the King James version of the Bible. In terms of the aspect of Buber's legacy that I have brought into Clear Space, it is all contained in the first part of *I and Thou*. The subsequent two parts relate more specifically to the way he links his relational philosophy to his conception of a deity. If you wanted to read more Buber, you might try *Between Man and Man* (also translated by Ronald Smith), but this would be much more of a project.

Carl Rogers was born in 1902 in Chicago and died in 1987 in San Diego. From an engineer father and a devout Pentecostal mother, he grew up a very disciplined person who is credited with being the first person to establish research as a discipline in the field of psychology and psychotherapy. He was a psychologist and held significant university and professional positions but, at a time when psychotherapy was dominated by psychoanalysis, developed a non-analytical humanistic approach to therapy. He moved away from using (psychological) method and formulated the person-centred approach, which held that it was the quality of the client-counsellor relationship, which was the prime therapeutic element. In simple form the nature of the relationship is defined in terms of the empathy, congruence and unconditional positive regard extended by the counsellor. He had a great interest in therapy for children, which was where he started, and the use of the therapeutic relationship in education, as well as being a renowned therapist. Later in life he extended the reach of his ideas into politics, and undertook work in Northern Ireland and South Africa. The person-centred approach has gone on developing since Rogers' death, and there is a very extensive bibliography. From among his own works, here are two, which are not specifically academic or teaching works: *Person to Person: the Problem of Being Human* (with alternate chapters by Barry Stevens on her passage through her own therapy) and *A Way of Being*, which touches on the application of his ideas in a number of settings and with many examples.

Eugene Gendlin was born in Vienna in 1926 but went to university in Chicago and has done most of his work in the USA. He is considered a philosopher as well as a psychotherapist and has developed theories around body awareness and our ongoing sense of 'a next step'. He believes that we carry our sense of our world and our being as a kind of bodily knowing. He developed the definition of 'felt sense' as something at the indistinct edge of awareness, beyond perception (which is cognitive) and with a conceptual feel. He worked alongside Carl Rogers at Chicago University and during this time set out Focusing as a method which could be used by therapists and also learnt by clients, as an aid to the process of change in psychotherapy. It was formulated as six steps, but was supported by a much more extensive academic analysis. Outside the psychological therapy profession, Focusing has developed as an activity in its own right spawning groups in Europe and America devoted to its teaching and practice. As a handbook, his original work for non-professional consumption, *Focusing*, is still perfectly valid, if sounding a little dated. However, there are many books by other authors, as a simple internet search will show. For a more in-depth but fairly demanding look at Gendlin's philosophy, there is *Thinking Beyond Patterns: Body, Language and Situations.*

About the Author

Simon Cole BA(Econ) MA(Counselling) MBACP(Snr Acc) has been a practising counsellor and therapist for 30 years. After working for several years with the Samaritans, he qualified as a counsellor at Newcastle University and gained a Masters degree with distinction from Ripon & York St John (then affiliated to Leeds University), later training with Joseph Zinker during his UK visits. Author of articles for counselling journals in the UK and Australia, he worked for many years within NHS primary and secondary care, whilst leading the counsellor training programmes at diploma level at Carlisle College. For the last seven years he has run a residential retreat centre in southwest France with his wife. The emphasis is on a therapy which picks up the natural rhythm of the surroundings and works with self-discovery through mindfulness and meditation, combined with creative counselling, music, poetry and writing. Mindfulness and meditation have for many years been a vital part of his life and have formed an increasingly significant part of his thera-peutic approach with the formalising of the Clear Space Meditation Path.

web: www.life-counselling.co.uk

email: simoncole.france@gmail.com